BEYOND
PEEK-A-BOO
AND
PAT-A-CAKE

ACTIVITIES FOR BABY'S FIRST YEAR

Evelyn Moats Munger and Susan Jane Bowdon

New Century Publishers, Inc.

Design by Bonnie Baumann

Illustrations by Jerry Warshaw

Copyright© 1980 by Evelyn Moats Munger and
Susan Jane Bowdon.
Cover design copyright© 1980 by New Century
Publishers, Inc. a subsidiary of New Century Education
Corporation.

Printing Code
13   14   15   16   17

Library of Congress Cataloging in Publication Data

Munger, Evelyn Moats, 1946-
  Beyond peek-a-boo and pat-a-cake.

  1. Infants. 2. Play. 3. Games. I. Bowdon,
Susan Jane, 1947- joint author. II. Title.
HQ774.M86   649'.122   80-13517
ISBN 0-8329-1439-8

Printed in United States of America

DEDICATION

To Dennis Munger for his good humor, support, and endurance.

To our parents, Georgia and Orin Moats and Jane Bowdon and Dr. Arthur Bowdon, for their confidence in their daughters.

Lastly to Marilyn Moats Kennedy, the sister who paved the way.

CONTENTS

FOREWORD

As a developmental psychologist who studies infants and carries out research in infant and child behavior, I was immediately struck by the unique features of this book. *Beyond Peek-a-Boo and Pat-a-Cake* combines current information from pediatrics and psychology about child development with a number of techniques for interacting with or stimulating an infant. These techniques do not require that the parents have a Ph.D. in child development or years of experience in dealing with infants; they do serve as very practical guides to help parents become sensitive observers and to accept a complementary rather than a passive ("I really don't know what to do") role during the early months.

Beyond Peek-a-Boo and Pat-a-Cake provides a basis for strengthening parents' confidence in their own abilities by explaining infant behavior in comprehensible terms; structuring approaches for essential infant-stimulation experiences through parent-child interactions using games, songs, and activities; and, perhaps most important for the parent, by suggesting workable solutions to the inevitable frustrations that accompany the normal development of any infant. The reader will be continually impressed by the many useful ideas and practical suggestions that the authors have provided to help parents cope with the realities of life with a baby. The ideas are ones that any reasonably intelligent, sensitive, and well-read parent might develop . . . if only he or she had a decade or so of experience with infants, didn't have to worry about other pressures, and weren't faced with the need for an immediate solution.

It is important to note that not all hints on management have to do with babies. Mothers and other caregivers count too, and necessary emphasis is placed on the caregiver's needs not only for time by oneself but also for contact with other adults.

This book promises to be one of the few really valuable sources to help parents learn about, survive with, and, above all, relax with and enjoy their new baby. I cannot think of a better way for parents to begin to adjust to the demands and respond to the delights of their infant than by using the ideas so well presented here.

William Fullard, Ph.D.
Associate Professor Human Development
Temple University

ACKNOWLEDGMENTS

Our appreciation to Elise Shiller for editorial help and to Judy Weglarz for hours of typing and retyping.

To our colleagues at the Temple University Day Care Center and the Durham Child Development Center for their willingness to share ideas and enthusiastic support.

To the Child Care Department, Temple University, School of Social Administration, for their encouragement.

And, to our friends and colleagues for their valuable suggestions and for their willingness to review our book:

Dr. William Fullard, Jr.
Dr. Barbara Gold
Dr. David Bechtel
Barbara Mollenhauer

INTRODUCTION

The abundance of research on infants in the last ten years has dispelled the once held notion of a baby's total helplessness. We now know that babies are highly responsive, eager to experience, and curious about the world around them. Studies have shown that not only can six-month-olds enjoy finger painting, but also that three-month-olds can, if they are given the opportunity, learn to control their crib mobiles through movement. *Beyond Peek-a-Boo and Pat-a-Cake* is designed to encourage parents, friends, and admirers of infants everywhere to follow their instincts and to watch, play with, talk to, stimulate, and, most of all, enjoy their babies. We hope that you will, with our help, learn just a little bit more about what your baby is truly capable of.

Beyond Peek-a-Boo and Pat-a-Cake was arranged chronologically for the sake of convenience. We wish to make it *very* clear that we are not trying to project a developmental timetable. Babies are people. Each infant has his or her own unique temperament, likes, dislikes, capabilities, and rate of growth. Because your baby may enjoy doing many of the activities out of sequence, we suggest that you skim through the entire book at the beginning of the year. What we have written is an idea book, a personalized journal, and a guide to help you learn along with your child during this first year.

We learned from experience that parents do not need another book describing babies, but that they desperately do need advice—specific suggestions about how to play, what to say, shortcuts for everyday routines, tips on handling babies in general.

For ease of readability we have used the masculine pronoun throughout the book. The masculine pronoun has been used exclusively in order to avoid cumbersome construction. It in no way implies that any activity or suggestion applies only to male infants.

Beyond Peek-a-Boo and Pat-a-Cake is divided into twelve chapters, one for each of the first twelve months of life. The first year of an infant's life is a demanding time physically and emotionally—for both child and parents. Each chapter of this book is organized to lead you from fun in the "Activities, Games, and Songs" section to the everyday basics of bathing, sleeping, feeding, and dressing and changing in the "Routine Times" section. The "Helpful Hints" section provides suggestions for living more efficiently with your baby; and the "Parents, Friends, and Admirers" section suggests ways of including others in your child's life. The "And for Yourself" features focus on activities and routines a new mother or caregiver might indulge in when Baby becomes too much.

We hope that *Beyond Peek-a-Boo and Pat-a-Cake* will be useful to parents, grandparents, baby-sitters, and caregivers alike. We hope that this book will provide you with many memorable moments with your baby.

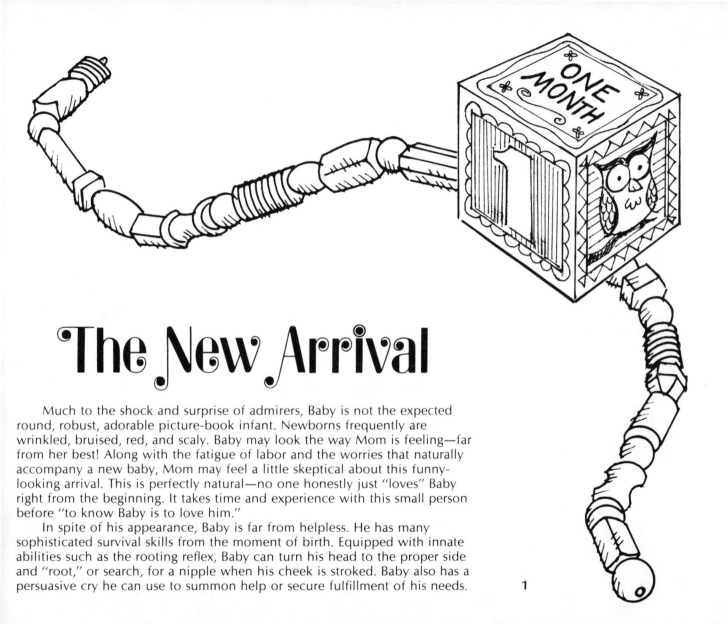

The New Arrival

Much to the shock and surprise of admirers, Baby is not the expected round, robust, adorable picture-book infant. Newborns frequently are wrinkled, bruised, red, and scaly. Baby may look the way Mom is feeling—far from her best! Along with the fatigue of labor and the worries that naturally accompany a new baby, Mom may feel a little skeptical about this funny-looking arrival. This is perfectly natural—no one honestly just "loves" Baby right from the beginning. It takes time and experience with this small person before "to know Baby is to love him."

In spite of his appearance, Baby is far from helpless. He has many sophisticated survival skills from the moment of birth. Equipped with innate abilities such as the rooting reflex, Baby can turn his head to the proper side and "root," or search, for a nipple when his cheek is stroked. Baby also has a persuasive cry he can use to summon help or secure fulfillment of his needs.

1

Although he seems sleepy much of the time, Baby is working to capacity to stabilize his vital systems. He is learning to breathe, digest food, and regulate his body temperature. Baby also has many environmental adjustments to make. No matter how comfortable one makes his surroundings, it is impossible to duplicate the womb.

At birth Baby can see well for from six to twelve inches from his body. He seems to prefer black and white patterns of any size or type to color in the items around him. Within a few weeks, as you play with Baby, you will notice that he can follow an object from side to center and back again. Now that Baby is alert for about one hour in ten, he is continually working with his eyes; he particularly enjoys focusing and will try to establish eye contact.

Baby possesses excellent hearing at birth. By the end of the first month, he will respond to voices, especially that of his primary caregiver. Although Baby loves attention, he will protect himself from overstimulation by simply not processing all the information that comes to him. When Baby is overtaxed, he will become suddenly more active or go to sleep; both mechanisms protect him from overstimulation.

The first few weeks with a new baby require that everyone involved get enough rest and a generous dose of tender loving care. This is a time of self-doubt for Baby's special people, who have been suddenly overwhelmed with an awesome responsibility. Even for those for whom parenting is not a new skill, it takes time to feel comfortable with a newborn again. As the weeks go by, you will become aware of how Baby signals for food, comfort, a change, or just peace and quiet. Familiarity will breed confidence, so take heart!

ACTIVITIES, GAMES, AND SONGS

Far from being a helpless little lump, Baby is born with many skills. The activity and game sections of this book will make the best use of these skills by suggesting fun learning experiences and enjoyable ways for Baby to practice what he knows.

Baby under Glass

Observing Baby is one of the most enjoyable and important activities for this first month. It's fascinating and exhilarating to watch this tiny being. Discover his uniqueness, his likes, dislikes, and abilities. Careful observation will alert you to the best time for play and learning. This can also be a restful time for recovering Moms and adjusting family members.

Blanket Play

It's not too early to allow your baby some freedom of movement and a change of surroundings. Encourage him to kick, stretch, and wiggle. If the room is warm, let Baby practice on a blanket on the floor.

A Ball for Baby

Hang a soft yarn pompom from Baby's crib mobile for him to watch. You may want to make more than one from different brightly colored yarns. Add some bells, too. Baby will enjoy the music.

Rattles

Put a rattle in Baby's hand, and watch to see if he can hold it for a few seconds. At this age, babies can let go of things only by chance, so you may have to remove the rattle after a short time. You can't expect too much grip this early.

Tape Magic

Place several three-inch strips of colored plastic tape on the crib sheet. Use bright colors for best results. Baby will enjoy trying to grasp and pick up the lines of color.

Beads and Bobbles

Wear a string of washable beads or a colorful pin. These will be of special interest to Baby as you hold him, and will enrich his visual environment. Baby's vision is best within twelve inches.

How Big?

A simple but enjoyable game to play is:

How big is Baby?
Soooooo big! (stretch arms)

How big is Baby?
Soooooo big! (stretch legs)

As Baby grows, so will his love for this game. Soon he will anticipate it with glee, raising his arms in delight. If you play this game regularly, Baby will gleefully respond to your questions with the proper motions by the time he is about ten months old.

Trips

A great trip to break up the day is a quick jaunt out the back door and once around the house. Do this several times a day. On a sunny day, try just sitting out in front of the house for a few minutes. You'll appreciate the change and Baby will get his introduction to the great outdoors.

Crazy Quilt

A crazy quilt can provide an exciting new environment of bright, intriguing colors for Baby. Maybe our ancestors knew more than we thought about infant delights. On the wall, under Baby when it's tummy time, or overhead at nap time, the patterns will intrigue him as he grows.

Snuggling

Slings (made of corduroy or denim) allow you to travel about your household without losing contact with Baby. These carriers hold Baby against your chest—a very comforting position. Easy instructions for making a baby sling can be found in many pattern books.

First Mobile

You can make Baby's first mobile. Keep it very simple and black and white. Research shows that newborns prefer the stark contrasts of black and white. Another study shows that babies also respond well to the human face.

Large circles, squares, triangles, and other geometric shapes readily appeal to infants. Position the mobile approximately eight to twelve inches from Baby. Make sure the mobile is safe for Baby. Always use short strings to hang the mobile so that he cannot become entangled in the strings. Change the mobile every week or so by adding shapes or switching their positions.

Best Time

Because you are taking cues from Baby, you already know when he is comfortable and relaxed. Allow him the opportunity to be himself and you'll know when he's ready to play. Be alert so you can join him in these happy moments.

The Young Cyclist

Even a young infant will enjoy a bit of cycling. Move his legs and bring his feet up to his body, one at a time or together. Do the same thing with his arms. This is an exercise either you or Baby can initiate.

Tone of Voice

How you speak to Baby matters. Very loud noises will startle him or cause him to cry. A smile and cheerful tone will make him coo or brighten. Soft tones will calm and soothe him. Hearing your voice is very important to his sense of well-being. Talk to him whenever you are together. Getting into the habit of talking to Baby early leads to better and earlier speech development.

Mmm Good

One of Baby's favorite pastimes is sucking his fingers. Sometimes he has difficulty finding his mouth. A little help will be appreciated, so give him "his hand." Sucking is very relaxing for Baby. Learning to use this skill for comfort is a first step toward self-reliance.

Set the Mood

Babies love mood music, too. Some babies, like adults, sleep best with background music. Try a variety of music—classical, jazz, blues, country and western—and notice Baby's responses.

Listen

Baby loves to listen to happy sounds. Add a wind chime to Baby's room. An inexpensive one can often be found in import shops.

What's Up?

Baby is often most alert when he is close to an upright position. Help him explore new things by holding him close enough to things that he can see using his good close-range vision. Moving about like this can be a game for Baby.

Where's Baby?

Place a diaper over Baby and say, "Where's Baby?" Raise the diaper and say, "There he is!" This favorite game becomes more and more fun as the child grows.

Mobile Mobile

Move the cradle gym or mobile you have hung at the level of the crib rails from side to side. This helps Baby notice change and practice focusing. Research suggests that by the end of the first month babies notice when objects have been so changed.

Looking Bonanza

Line the crib or bassinet with bright simple pictures for Baby to look at. He can see these pictures very well because they are close, and he will spend many happy moments studying them carefully.

Minimassage

Baby will enjoy a minimassage. Use a little lukewarm baby oil or baby powder. If you decide to use baby powder, avoid Baby's inhalation of clouds of talc by pouring or shaking the powder into your hand before applying. Start at the neck and work down, talking or humming as you go. This promotes body awareness and feels good.

Light On

Light is an exciting stimulus to an infant. A dim lamp or nightlight will provide Baby with an opportunity to look around his bed and his room. It is never too early for Baby to practice entertaining himself before sleeping and upon waking.

Rocking

The rhythmic movement a baby feels when being rocked is very comforting. Research suggests that most babies respond best to being held upright as they are soothed using the motion achieved by an old-fashioned rocking chair. Some rocking speeds are better than others; medium to high seems best. If you do not have a rocker, consider buying one.

For other hints on handling a fussy baby, see Appendix A.

Chase the Light

A small flashlight can be the beginning of a "chase the light" game. For fun, tape colored cellophane over the light; red and yellow are Baby's favorites. Catch Baby's eye and slowly move the light from one side to another. It will take some practice, but you will soon see Baby's eyes track the colored light.

Sing That Lullaby

A very special time in these early weeks of life can involve singing some soon-to-be favorite songs as you cuddle and rock Baby.

The traditional lullaby "Rock-a-Bye Baby" goes like this:

Rock-a-bye baby, in the treetop,
When the wind blows, the cradle will rock.
When the bough breaks, the cradle will fall,
And down will come baby,
Cradle and all.

Maybe you'd prefer a show tune such as "Lullaby of Broadway," or a favorite popular song. Better yet, make up your own. See "Ode to Baby" in the Chapter 2 section on "Parents, Friends, and Admirers" for tips on writing baby poems.

Shimmer, Sparkle, and Spin

Sparkly or shiny objects often catch the eye of a newborn. Make a simple object out of crumpled aluminum foil suspended by string, ribbon, or dental floss.

ROUTINE TIMES

If you are convinced that *nothing* is routine with an infant, you are probably correct, especially during this first month. However, there are certain things that must be done every day and certain needs that must be met.

As you grow to know your child, you will become aware of his preferences and internal timetable. Throughout this book, "Routine Times" will deal with day-to-day issues such as feeding, toileting, bathing, dressing, sleeping, and so on.

BATHING

Baby's first baths are far more frightening for Baby's friends than for him. There are many ways to bathe an infant. We have included some suggestions, but certainly not all. The important thing is that you find one method with which you feel comfortable so that you can enjoy bathtimes with Baby.

Frog Position

Use just a little water, and place Baby in a frog position, your hand under his chest and his head on your arm.

Alternatives

Place Baby in his infant seat and then in a small basin with very little water. This leaves both your hands free to work.

Rather than kneeling and bending over the bathtub, try the sink. You'll find it's a perfect size for Baby, and a lot less precarious for both of you.

Or consider a sponge bath until you have gained confidence and the umbilical cord has come off. Better yet, have your mother or friend help the first few times, for moral support.

Warranty: Your baby is fully guaranteed not to break for one full year. With reasonable care these models last a lifetime.

Bath Bucket

Remember the small plastic bucket you used to carry your bathroom gear to the bathroom when you were in college? This is a great way to store Baby's things for bathing, assuring that you won't need something you didn't bring.

Baby's Reaction

Here's a space to record Baby's initial reactions to his earliest baths.

_____

_____

_____

_____

SLEEPING

As with every other aspect of Baby's adjustment to life, sleep needs and patterns may undergo many changes before stabilizing. Baby's pattern may be as much as eighteen to twenty hours per day or as few as twelve for the first few weeks. Each infant is unique.

Young Sleeper's Chart

	A.M.	P.M.	NIGHT
S.	_____	_____	_____
M.	_____	_____	_____
T.	_____	_____	_____
W.	_____	_____	_____
TH.	_____	_____	_____
F.	_____	_____	_____
S.	_____	_____	_____

Carriage Sleeping

Use Baby's carriage as a second baby bed. When Baby naps, you can simply wheel it to an adjoining room. This will save a recovering mother or a busy caregiver many steps.

If you live in a two-story house, keep the carriage on the first floor so that you can easily hear Baby when he cries.

Color

Babies like color and pattern in their cribs. Sheets, bumpers, blankets, and pajamas should be bright and printed. Pastels appeal only to adults.

Extra Bed for Baby

Need an extra bed or sleeping space? Try a padded bureau drawer. Betty Ford claims all her children used them for the first few months.

Noise

Babies' sleep patterns are a highly individual matter. Some settle into a predictable routine; others will keep you guessing. Many infants can sleep through all but the loudest bangs and jolts, so go ahead and converse, use various appliances, and know that members of the household need not tiptoe and whisper. It's better to begin this way. It's also fairer to anxious siblings.

FEEDING

Bubbling (Burping)

Not all babies require bubbling or burping, but some need attention before, during, and after feeding. You will quickly come to know your own infant's needs.

Bubbling usually produces a quick burp that gets rid of any air that may have collected in Baby's

stomach during feeding. Try one of these three techniques, positioning a clean towel between you and Baby.
1. Lay Baby on his tummy over your lap. Supporting his head with your hand, turn Baby's head to one side and gently pat him on the back. This is a good technique to use with newborns. Remember, easy does it.
2. A sitting position works well for some babies. Using both your hands to support head, neck, shoulders, and back, Baby can be rocked or patted.
3. Try rubbing up and down along Baby's spine, especially between the shoulder blades, while he rests over your hand or shoulder.

Breast or Bottle

Regardless of which manner of feeding you choose, most babies will not only survive but thrive. Essential to the success of either method is the manner in which you carry out each feeding. Feeding is, after all, a high point of Baby's life. Beyond food, it is a social exchange of affection.

Bottle-feeding parents should be sure to cuddle and hug Baby while he drinks. Mutual satisfaction is the goal. This is one of the many ways Baby and you get to know each other.

Mothers who are nursing can get information and support from

> La Leche League International
> 9616 Minneapolis Ave.
> Franklin Park, IL 60131

First Month Feeding Chart

A.M.

_____ _____

_____ _____

_____ _____

_____ _____

P.M.

_____ _____

_____ _____

_____ _____

_____ _____

Sucking

One way an infant can reduce tension and comfort himself is to suck his fist and later his fingers. Because the mouth is really at the center of Baby's world, sucking is as important as feeding or nourishment.

Extra Satisfaction

If your child enjoys a pacifier, fine; if not, that's fine, too. No research we know of suggests that use of a pacifier is harmful for infants. Some theorists indicate pacifiers may have psychologically beneficial effects. Only Baby knows, and he's not telling.

Both Sides Now

Feed and change Baby from alternate sides. This helps him develop a sense of self.

DRESSING AND CHANGING

"Shape" Your Surface

Instead of buying a changing table, cut and cover your own. Use a piece of foam rubber two to four inches thick. Personalize this work surface by cutting the foam rubber into a creative shape. Cover it with cheery printed oilcloth, contact paper, or a vinyl tablecloth. Place on top of a low dresser or on the counter of a large bathroom vanity or cabinet.

In Vogue

Designer fashions have limited value in the early weeks of life. Any item of clothing made of special fabric or of intricate design will prove impractical.

The fact is that Baby may need a complete change of clothes with each fresh diaper. This could mean as many as eight outfits a day.

Keep newborns' togs simple, washable, durable, and free from fasteners that might be gummed or swallowed. Many babies dislike shirts or outfits that must be pulled over the head. Snaps in front are the answer. Babies like the loose look.

So that outfits need not be discarded after three or four weeks, starting size should be size 6 months.

Tips for the Changing Table

Don't wait to gather all your supplies together—every pin and washcloth. The prepared caregiver finds that the business of diapering will be shared by others when everything is close at hand. Organization counts, so don't delay.

Different Folds for Different Folks

There are three basic techniques for folding cotton diapers. Try any or all to determine which gives you the best coverage for your infant. Remember that boys need extra thickness in the front, girls more coverage in the back.

The Square is a good folding technique to try with a newborn, especially if the baby is on his back much of the time. This style has less flexibility in adjustment than do the other two. It's the loosest style, good for a summer day.

The Kite is a particularly neat-fitting diaper for a boy because there is more up front where it counts. Kite-folded diapers fit well inside plastic pants.

The Oblong provides the most complete coverage front and rear, but tends to appear a bit bulky. This style is an excellent choice for night use.

Diaper Service?

If you can afford it, a diaper service for the first seven months is certainly the luxury of luxuries. Remember that most babies need eight to ten diapers per day.

Disposable diapers, another option for cutting your work load, are more costly than cloth diapers.

HELPFUL HINTS

Learning from others' experiences can certainly make life with a new baby easier and more pleasant. The "Helpful Hints" sections of the book are designed to help you use your time and materials more efficiently. They are a compilation of tricks and shortcuts others have found valuable.

Reminder

Yes, women have been having babies since the year one. And things *have* improved considerably in this modern age. Still, having a newborn to look after is an enormous undertaking. So remember to *ask for help.* You can make this easier and more rewarding for all by developing a list of small errands and tasks to be done.

It matters that you are doing more than just coping. What makes you happy, secure, and relaxed?

Ring, Ring

If you have several extension phones, make copies of a list of numbers you use most frequently and place one next to each extension. For example,

Doctors _____

_____

Best Friends _____
(Advice)

_____

Relatives _____

_____

Baby-sitters _____

_____

Get to know businesses or services that pick up and deliver—that difference is worth your money.

Grocery store _____

Laundry/cleaners _____

Diaper service _____

Drugstore/pharmacy _____

Bookstore _____

Temporary cleaning help _____

Dinner on Tap

Food may be the farthest thing from your mind, but then again. . . ? A week's worth of dinners will allow you a social meal with family and friends. For instance, spaghetti sauce to be used for chili, chicken cacciatore, and spaghetti can be made in bulk and frozen. With a little planning, many basic meals made in quantity can be varied to provide a few days' worth of delicious meals. Write out complete menus, attach recipes or page numbers cited. Keep a file of these menus handy in your kitchen.

Energy Cycle

Mother or not, this new baby is putting you through some major changes. You are a different person. Anyone involved at any extended level with an infant, will discover that pace is everything.

Rest is a number one priority. So rest. The "found moments" when Baby is resting will make a difference when you need to gear up to cook, clean, or collect yourself enough to face the latest low-level crisis.

Matters of diet, recreation, and health are of prime importance. Taking care of your health, physical and mental, is essential to your good relationship with Baby.

Cheap, Cheap

With the excitement of a new arrival, remember to buy special equipment only as a last resort. Think about borrowing and swapping. Buy only if all else fails. Check your neighborhood newspaper for good buys on slightly used baby equipment. Seasonal considerations will influence the number of items you will need.

Night-Light

Eliminate late evening stumbles by placing simple night-lights in dark hallways and rooms. Some nice ones recently spotted had shells and sand dollars glued in front of the bulb. Very low energy night-lights are now available.

Letting Go

Households will endure despite dust, fuzz, bathtub rings, and dirty windows. Your needs are of the utmost significance. Adjustment is the key word. Hassle yourself as little as possible; let go of some of those perfectionist standards. If you do not have regular cleaning help, this is where you can guiltlessly splurge this month!

A Cup of Comfort

Install a small (single-cup size) electric teapot in Baby's room. When feedings continue longer than you had anticipated, a mug of tea, bouillon, or hot chocolate can be very relaxing. Stock up and enjoy.

Fast Eats

A list of fast-food restaurants, especially those that deliver, can be a real time-saver. Post the list on the refrigerator door for a convenient alternative on a day when cooking is all but impossible.

Peace of Mind

Since 1973, all full-sized baby cribs have been required by law to meet the safety standards of the Consumer Product Safety Commission. These standards are very stringent requirements and do ensure product safety. If you plan to use a second-hand crib made before 1973, you will want to check its features against these safety standards.

Things to watch for include distance between slats (no more than 23 in.); secure locking devices on crib sides, ones that an older child cannot move; nontoxic, lead-free paint; and safe metal hardware. The mattress should fit snugly into the frame; if you can fit more than two fingers between the mattress and the frame, the mattress is too small.

Health Record

An up-to-date chart of all Baby's medical information can be invaluable when faced with an emergency, a change of doctor, or a move to a new location.

	DATE	DATE
DPT (diphtheria, whooping cough, tetanus)	———	———
	———	———
	———	
Polio	———	———
Smallpox	———	———
Typhoid	———	———
Mumps	———	———
Measles	———	———
Rubella	———	———
Tuberculin Test	———	———

Frantic

Baby's first illness will be very frightening. Don't panic. First, gather the facts. Then, call the doctor. Facts to know:

Symptoms ————————————————

   (diarrhea, vomiting, appearance)

Baby's mood ————————————————

Sleep pattern ————————————————

   (last twelve hours)

Eating pattern ————————————————

   (how much, what, when)

Temperature ————————————————

   (how taken)

First Doctor

One of the most important relationships is the one between you and your child's doctor. This can be a long relationship and merits investigation, time, and thought. The right physician is a lifelong friend, counselor, and resource.

Baby's Physician

Name ————————————————

Address ————————————————

Phone: Office _____

Home _____

Office hours _____

Hospital affiliation(s)

_____

Paint

Start out right and think *latex*. Water-based latex paints are nontoxic, easy to apply, and easy to clean up.

Beauty Parlor

Clip Baby's nails while he's asleep. This is a good way to accomplish a tricky task.

Organize

If you need to gather and group small items, consider using a set of colorful canisters, graduated plastic boxes, metal cans, or wicker baskets. By doing so, you can keep all those necessary but dangerously small items out of sight and reach. Babyproof now!

Odors

Help Baby to put his best foot forward. You may be immune to Baby's smells, but others are not. Besides keeping him clean, you will need a plan for handling soiled clothes and diapers. Make sure that

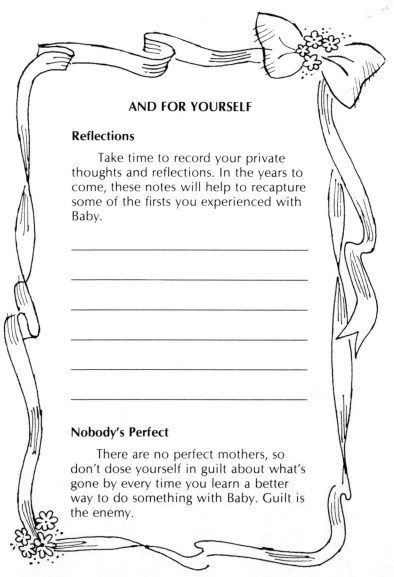

AND FOR YOURSELF

Reflections

Take time to record your private thoughts and reflections. In the years to come, these notes will help to recapture some of the firsts you experienced with Baby.

_____

_____

_____

_____

_____

_____

Nobody's Perfect

There are no perfect mothers, so don't dose yourself in guilt about what's gone by every time you learn a better way to do something with Baby. Guilt is the enemy.

diapers are placed in containers with tight-fitting lids. Empty frequently.

Air Fresheners

Use room deodorizers to keep your environment pleasant. The commercial brands that attach to the wall are especially convenient. Whatever you choose, remember to place these dispensers up and out of the way of little hands.

Crying

Yes, babies do cry, often and loudly. Although not a solution, it may help to know that crying does indicate something. Frequency of crying will begin to diminish in the next few weeks.

Most educators feel that you can't spoil an infant. In fact, research has found that prompt response to Baby's crying results in a decrease, rather than an increase, in crying.

Hang on. Your patience and tolerance will be rewarded.

First Cold

When Baby gets his first cold, make him more comfortable by doing the following.

Use a cold-mist humidifier. Also try raising one end of the crib several notches so Baby's head will be elevated slightly; you can also accomplish this by placing bricks or books under the front feet of the crib.

Give him lots of tender care and fluids and follow your doctor's advice. Do try not to become overly distressed.

The Old Rope Trick

If you have a rocking cradle or a buggy, place it near your bed and attach a string. When Baby cries, pull the string and rock Baby—this helps you get the rest you need too. (See Chapter 2, "Routine Times: Crib Springs" for a way to convert your crib into a rocking crib by changing the casters.)

Hot Flashes

Newborns are more sensitive to heat than to cold. Keep Baby warm, but don't overdo it. Many babies are kept so well dressed that they suffer from prickly heat rash or from the "drowsies." Experiences in other countries have shown that infants stay healthier in cooler rooms. So do adults.

Quick Slips

If you would rather have cotton closest to Baby's skin, consider slipping colorful pillowcases over the changing pad. These easy-to-clean cases provide Baby with new and stimulating things to look at, as well as a cool, crisp touch.

Extra Bed

If Baby is sleeping in his own room, furnish it with a cot or an extra bed for Mom or Dad. On those long, fussy nights (and there are bound to be a few), parents can catnap during Baby's restful moments.

Someone Sleeps

Many parents we know claim that the only viable method for coping with a baby's erratic sleeping needs and patterns is a rotation of duty. The one-night-off, one-night-on, or one-feeding-off, one-feeding-on procedure allows at least one parent to sleep.

Fathers of nursing babies can still help out. Dad can get up and retrieve Baby, change him, and bring him to bed for his feeding.

PARENTS, FRIENDS, AND ADMIRERS

The "Parents, Friends, and Admirers" sections of the book address the needs of Baby's best friends: parents, grandparents, siblings, admirers, and caregivers. It includes ideas for them to use, things to buy, ways to help, and plans for good times.

Let Me See

Everyone, even people you thought would never know or care, seems to have heard about *this* baby and decided to call or visit. Although flattering, it can be overwhelming. Don't be afraid to schedule these admirers and well-wishers.

You can say no without guilty feelings or lengthy explanations. Time flies and soon you and Baby will not be as sensitive.

Door Note

A note on the door, "We'll be delighted to see visitors after _____," is one way of letting neighbors know when to come.

Operators

Take the phone off the hook for part of the day, or use an answering service to relay your message of "good times to call," along with a little news about the new arrival. This can be a great service to everyone.

Flag Pole Alert

To announce the new arrival, hoist a fabric flag in front of the house to alert friends that Baby has indeed arrived. This banner can then be used to indicate good times to visit or stay away.

Chain Announcement

Write a letter to your best friend with all the information on the new baby; have this friend start the chain to send from friend to friend. Each person can add his or her best wishes and whatever new information has been gathered. When the letter is finally returned to you, it will be a warm and cherished keepsake about Baby, drafted with love by dear friends.

For the Teacher

Let your class or neighborhood help you announce the new arrival. Before delivery, have students draw pictures of the new "baby and company" on postcards to be used for the announcements.

If you're not a teacher, consider enlisting the artistry of kids in your neighborhood. This is one way of discovering just how this baby is viewed by young friends.

Small Town

Place your announcement as an advertisement in the local newspaper. It's a sure way to spread the good news.

Siblings

Even if you have spent time preparing children for Baby's arrival, expect times when they are less than enthusiastic about sharing their world with an infant.

Reading stories that reflect their feelings can provide siblings with a guilt-free outlet. It will also give them opportunity to discuss and decide ways in which brothers and sisters can be involved happily with Baby.

Some books we like are:
Peter's Chair by Ezra Jack Keats
Nobody Asked Me If I Wanted a Baby Sister by Martha Alexander
We are Having a Baby by Vicki Holland
The Berenstain Bears' New Baby by Stan and Jan Berenstain
William's Doll by Charlotte Zolotow

Special Call

Having Mom in the hospital can be a disturbing experience for young children. Hearing her voice over the phone can make a real difference and quickly assure them that everything is just fine. Or have Mom leave a happy cassette recording, made with the child, for playing during a lonely time.

Thank You

Looking for a different way to thank the gang from work? A blow-up poster of Baby surrounded by the nice gifts he received is a great way to say thanks for everything and to introduce Baby.

Grandparents Only

Baby's first baby-sitters will probably be his grandparents. Only they can give this special gift to new parents who need a break but are too uncomfortable to leave their young infant with just anyone. Grandparents can provide new parents with renewed confidence and necessary moral support. They can be an endless source of information.

Little Red Riding Hood

Little Red Riding Hood had the right idea. A great gift for the exhausted parents of the new arrival is a "bring-in-dinner" left on the doorstep. Complete the package with plastic stemware, wine, and a candle or two. You might even add a little mood music in the form of a favorite album or tape.

Mysterious Maid

Your time can be a very helpful gift. Doing the dishes or the laundry or fixing a few meals that can be warmed up when needed can certainly be a relief to a woman too tired to do the work herself but concerned about how the rest of her family is faring.

Gifts Received

GIFT	GIVER	DATE THANKED

Hints

A short pleasant call from a thoughtful grandparent can brighten the day for a recuperating Mom. Include a little news and perhaps an invitation for dinner later this month.

The "Stork" Truth

From the first moment of birth, everyone knows who Baby looks like. No one will believe us, but the truth is Baby only really looks like himself.

Real Class

Got a classy baby? Consider a printed "At Home" card for the debut.

Baby's Name

after the seventeenth
of May 19 ___

29 East Penn Street
Philadelphia, PA

New Moms

Besides jewels, furs, and flowers, new Moms are receptive to the following gifts:
1. A best-seller to read in the tub
2. New lipsticks, nail polish
3. Flashy running shoes or new street skates to provide an incentive
4. A sexy but loose-fitting nightgown with a lovely neckline
5. A favorite record album
6. Colorful sheets to brighten her corner
7. A comfy rocking chair you found at a yard sale and covered with a new coat of cheerful paint

Photographs

There is nothing more valuable than early pictures of famous and successful people.

Start immediately to capture Baby's formative months. If Baby's parents are not shutterbugs, photos can be a wonderful present.

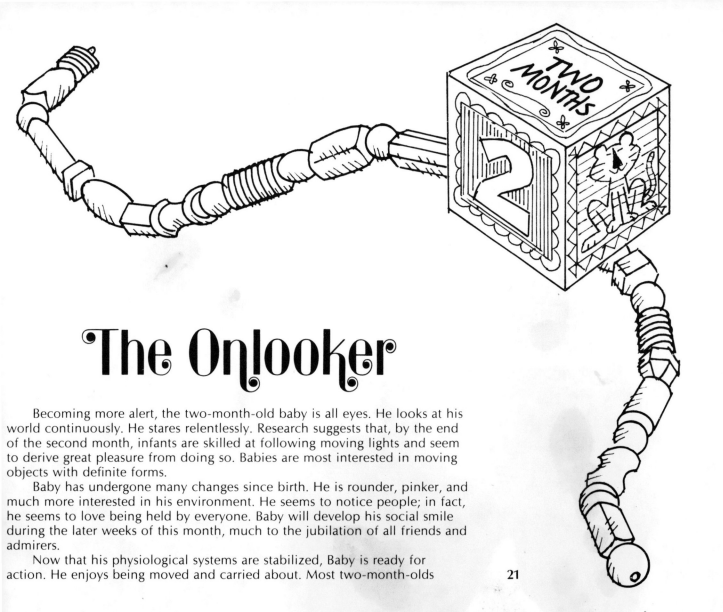

The Onlooker

Becoming more alert, the two-month-old baby is all eyes. He looks at his world continuously. He stares relentlessly. Research suggests that, by the end of the second month, infants are skilled at following moving lights and seem to derive great pleasure from doing so. Babies are most interested in moving objects with definite forms.

Baby has undergone many changes since birth. He is rounder, pinker, and much more interested in his environment. He seems to notice people; in fact, he seems to love being held by everyone. Baby will develop his social smile during the later weeks of this month, much to the jubilation of all friends and admirers.

Now that his physiological systems are stabilized, Baby is ready for action. He enjoys being moved and carried about. Most two-month-olds

21

enjoy vehicular travel. The trusty baby swing can begin to be a pleasure for Baby and grown-ups starting this month; it can be a lifesaver for the difficult-to-soothe baby.

Baby can now hold up his head and grasp things voluntarily; he may even try swiping at objects. Baby will show his delight and excitement when new objects are presented to him by cooing and making throaty noises.

Caregivers and parents will find Baby's behavior easier to predict. His feedings will be more regular, as will be his sleeping patterns.

There are more opportunities for getting to know Baby now that he stays awake for longer periods of time. When he's played with, he may even perform a little for his friends. He prefers people to toys, and will clearly discriminate among individual voices. Being touched, held, and fed are still Baby's favorite activities.

ACTIVITIES, GAMES, AND SONGS

Baby is delighted by a variety of sensations, sounds, lights, and textures. This month try some activities that will enhance his growing awareness of his body.

Sounds Like

Babies are attracted to noises. Make sure that your child's world is full of interesting sounds. Not only should toys be attractive, touchable, and mouthable, they should also provide the extra dimension of sound.

Cool Breeze

Before throwing out that paper-towel or tissue tube, consider Baby and paint it. He will enjoy the cool stream of air that you can direct toward his tummy or leg, etc. A large straw or piece of plastic tubing would also work well and help Baby to focus on different parts of his body.

A Ball for Baby

Baby would probably enjoy a cloth ball that tinkles. Such a ball is easy to make from assorted cloth scraps and jingle bells. Make sure bells are permanently embedded inside the toy.

Clothesline Art

A great eye delighter is this simple crib item made from elastic cord and several one-inch bulldog paper clips. Thread the clips onto the cord and stretch it across Baby's crib; tie it to the rails on either side. From the clips, hang anything and everything you think might interest Baby. Consider a feather, flower, ribbon, bow, or a small stuffed toy. What is especially nice about this item is the ease with which the assortment can be changed.

Dancing Face

Direct the gaze of that wide-eyed baby by making him a fantastic face! You can use a paper plate or styrofoam meat tray as a base. The best part is up to you. A simple design should include all the basics. Use a bit of colorful yarn for hair. Present to Baby. This cheerful face could be hung within Baby's view or danced before his eyes by a parent or admirer.

Are You Singing?

Keep those tunes simple, but keep singing; oldies are still goodies for Baby. Remember:

"Twinkle, Twinkle Little Star"
"You Are My Sunshine"

Finger Fancy

How about trying this one with Baby, fondling each finger as you go along? Either recite it or make up your own tune.

This is little Tommy Thumb,
   round and smooth as any plum;
This is busy Peter Pointer,
   surely he's a double-jointer;
This is mighty Toby Tall,
   he's the biggest one of all;
This is dainty Robin Ring,
   he's too fine for anything;
And this little wee one, maybe,
   surely he's the Finger Baby;
All the five we've counted now,
Busy fingers in a row,
All together they work best,
Each one helping all the rest.

Soft Sounds

Whisper, whisper, whisper. A sweet nothing is something of a surprise and a treat for Baby. Some parents report that this is a sure way to comfort a fussy baby.

Sing Along

Do join in on Baby's own songs, too. Imitate his every sound and then wait for his response. Babies like this game.

Head Lifts

Babies need time to practice raising their heads. Place Baby on his tummy and encourage him to look up at toys you dance before his eyes. Using brightly colored toys that also make a noise gives Baby that much more incentive to see what's up.

Voices

Try changing your tone. Notice the difference? Babies are soothed by a high voice. They are attracted to a voice that is low in tone.

Centerfold

Snap! . . . whether this is the first baby or not, take lots of pictures. How about one of Baby at play or with his favorite playmates?

Pulling Power

Since birth, Baby has had quite a grasp. Recent studies demonstrate that infants have up to two pounds of power in each hand. Up to now, Baby has been able to "hang on," but this survival skill will begin to disappear at around six weeks of age. Be sure that you support Baby when you bring him to a sitting position by pulling him up by his fists or shoulders.

Fist to Fingers

Baby's fist may be opening up a bit now to reveal fingers. Do things together with those hands. Wiggle the fingers; call attention to them. Wave your own. Touch, clap, shake, and tickle his palm.

Footing Around

A paint project for you and Baby to begin now is footprinting. Using a colorful stamp pad, a bit of water-based paint or any other substance (even chocolate pudding) as a medium, collect a sample every two or three months for the first three years of life. These prints can become a developmental graphic. Each print might contain comments on Baby's size, and perhaps a special anecdote.

Name

As you sing a tune, or play with rhymes, remember to include Baby's name whenever possible. This is just another important way to personalize your playtime together. The best songs are those you make up just for Baby.

Puppet Power

New and interesting faces can be provided for Baby through the use of puppets. A good investment, the puppets will be a source of delight throughout his childhood.

Porcupines and Rhinos

Prickly porcupines, frogs, rhinos, fish with rubber scales, and other toys designed for puppies provide interesting textures, and are especially easy for infants to hold. These soft, sturdy toys don't object to being mouthed. They also make delightful squeaking noises at unexpected moments.

Swipe and Grab

Move a ball of crushed foil to a place where Baby can practice beginning to swipe. Add to Baby's pleasure by concealing a small bell inside the ball.

Swing Easy

You may want to try a commercially available wind-up swing. It's a favorite of babies at this stage. The swing also relaxes many babies at fussy times. For extra fun, attach a suction-cup toy to the tray of the swing so Baby has things to swipe at as he flies through the air.

Wrist Wear

You like jewelry; why shouldn't Baby? How about bangles made of colorful cotton braid or ribbon? Baby will admire his lovely wrists and become more aware of his body.

Disco Duck

Make those feet move. Keep the beat. Baby will enjoy some passive exercises done to a lively beat.

Ceiling Sights

Baby spends most of his crib time looking at the ceiling and the walls of his crib. Why not put your efforts where they count?

African, Mexican, or other ethnic wall hangings and small rugs have marvelous colors and patterns for Baby's gaze. A Southwestern God's Eye or a baby banner of your own design can be entertaining when hung from the ceiling or wall near Baby's crib.

Joyride

Place Baby in his infant seat and then place the seat on top of your washing machine during the spin cycle. The gentle vibration and humming noise will delight Baby during this short joyride, while you're standing by.

A Little Outdoors

If the weather is too bad to take Baby outside, bring a little of the great outdoors in to Baby. Snip a branch from a tree or bush and place it near Baby, where he can carefully study it and smell its freshness. A small bird or colorful butterfly from the dime store can add extra interest.

Design Thought

Researchers emphasize that Baby's view is not the same as ours. When designing mobiles and crib toys, remember that Baby is looking up and sees the bottom of the objects placed over him.

Not Us

One researcher reports that if babies are left in cribs or playpens for long periods during their alert, learning times, their sense of curiosity can be severely crippled by the time they are fourteen or fifteen months old. Not so for our baby. With all the stimulation he's getting, his lack of curiosity will not be a concern!

ROUTINE TIMES

BATHING

By now, Baby is two feet long and probably enjoying his bath. If you use washcloths, the baby-sized ones are more convenient, but regular-sized towels are fine. To keep a young wiggler from sliding around, place a towel in the bottom of the sink or plastic tub.

A Bath Toy

Cut a clean sponge into a shape for Baby to hang onto and squeeze. Baby will enjoy watching and touching this textured item, which jumps back into shape upon being released.

Infants Only

Strip Baby and let him kick and wiggle. Total body freedom, at least for a few minutes before the bath, is an activity often reserved only for the young. Baby deserves the opportunity to learn about his environment and body in many different ways. Wearing only one's birthday suit does feel much different than a creeper, and can be exhilarating.

Stack-ups

To streamline the bathtime ritual, organize by the stack method. This arrangement begins as the laundry is sorted. On the bottom of the stack, put Baby's outer garment, then his undershirt. Next, add Baby's diaper, and top off with his towel.

Towel-Time Rhyme

Try this with Baby after each bath as you dry him. Dry the parts of his body in conjunction with the poem. He will soon look forward to his after-bath game. Our three-year-old friend Carla can recite it herself.

After a Bath

After my bath, I try, try, try
To wipe myself till I'm dry, dry, dry.
Hands to wipe, and fingers and toes,
And two wet legs and a shiny nose.
Just think how much less time I'd take
If I were a dog and could shake, shake, shake.

Warm Oil Treatment

Place a container of baby oil in the tub as you begin the bathing routine. Taking the chill off the oil will add to the pleasure of Baby's after-bath rubdown.

SLEEPING

Routine

Babies do get attached to specific toys and their crib environment. Making Baby feel at home with his blanket and special things can help in establishing sleeping patterns. A song or special pat can create a napping routine that Baby will grow to associate with rest.

Cozy Corner

Baby does not need the entire space of his crib for sleeping. Some babies feel more comfortable and sleep better in a cozier space. If this is true of your child, use only part of the crib and place some of Baby's soft cuddly toys in the corners to decrease the space.

"Belly Down"

All babies have preferred sleeping positions. Be observant and learn Baby's preferred position. This can make naptime easier.

Settle Down

Give Baby a chance to settle himself for rest. Some babies routinely cry before they drift off to sleep. Of course, you'll check to see if there is a problem. Then, watch a clock to reassure yourself that this crying lasts for only a few minutes.

Nightgear for Kickers

Keep little kickers warm throughout the night by dressing them in sleeping bags, sacks, or jumpsuits. These measures will assure you that Baby is cozy and help reduce the number of trips you make to the nursery "just to check" on his coverage.

Baby Bed Bumpers

These cheery devices not only add warmth and eye appeal to a crib, they are also a great safety precaution. Bed bumpers come in prints, colors, and even clear inflatable plastic. If you enjoy sewing, you may want to make your own out of fabric-covered foam rubber bolsters.

Crib Springs

The casters on Baby's crib can be removed and replaced with a set of specially made springs. These springs allow the crib to be rocked; they also permit Baby to bounce the crib and jostle his mobiles himself.

Research has shown that infants will try to control the movement of their mobiles and, if successful, will try to perfect their act. Having made the association that their movements caused the mobiles to sway, these infants enjoy entertaining themselves.

Crib springs can be purchased at any store carrying infant furniture (approximately $6.00 per set).

FEEDING

Atmosphere

Feeding is an important time, Baby's favorite. A pleasant atmosphere is something worth planning for, for both you and Baby.

Think about yourself in a restaurant; low lights, sparkling conversation, and mood music can make all the difference. More is happening here than just the satisfaction of hunger. Mealtimes are traditionally happy, sharing times among family and friends. Get off to a good start with Baby!

Burps . . .

Older babies can now rest their heads comfortably on someone's shoulder for bubbling. Massage Baby's back gently. Cover your shoulder with a bold-colored towel to enhance Baby's widening visual experience. By now, Baby has a preferred position for burping. It is

_____

Preferred Position/Date

I'm Ready

Baby will begin to anticipate feeding time. He may make sucking noises—real smacking sounds to let you know that he is preparing himself. He will probably be able to both suck and stare, a new development for Baby.

Sucking

One way to determine if Baby is really aware of you is to observe his sucking patterns. The curious baby will stop briefly to consider something and then focus his gaze on an object of interest. The contented baby sucks because sucking is a source of genuine pleasure.

Researchers say that the happiest babies suck the most. Babies will try nipples, their fingers, their thumbs, their toys, and their bedding. By sucking, babies can reduce muscular tension and calm themselves.

Pacifiers

To the young infant, there is not a great deal of difference between a thumb and a pacifier. Both soothe and satisfy the need to suck. Although research suggests that neither is harmful, pacifiers are less likely than thumbs to cause orthodontic problems. Pacifiers are frequently discarded by Baby at about six months of age.

DRESSING AND CHANGING

Hooks and Knobs

Place a set of colorful enamel hooks and knobs on the wall near Baby's changing table or dresser. Arrange them in an interesting pattern. These are handy for you now; later, when Baby becomes a "me-do" toddler, they can be moved to a lower position and continue to be useful.

Instant Shelves

A small shelf above Baby's changing area can be indispensable. Try a wicker or stainless steel bathroom shelf. These are easy to hang and require only two holes that can be covered by a picture when you are past the changing table stage.

Head to Toe

An attractive and fun way to store some of Baby's clothes is to use tiered lettuce baskets, which can be found in gourmet shops. These are so handy in the kitchen or pantry, why not try them in Baby's room? Or use graduated wicker baskets. Hang several from cup hooks; fill each with a complete change of clothing, starting with shirts and working your way down. You can quickly dress Baby from head to toe. The baskets are easy to see and reach and require little space.

Up and Out

After you change your baby, you might do a few exercises. Raise his arms up and out. Legs, too. Baby will think this is fun. Talk to him and praise his wiggles and kicks.

HELPFUL HINTS

Concentrate on getting to know your baby rather than on having all the right answers.

Everything in Its Place

An attractive, organized way to store Baby's paraphernalia is to keep it in a shoe storage bag. Hang one by the changing table, and perhaps another near the bathtub.

Shake, Shake, Shake

If you are using cornstarch instead of baby powder, a large salt shaker might make a handy dispenser.

Magic Box

Now is the time to become a collector of all the noncommercial toys and objects (feathers to fabric, balls to bells) that you'll introduce to Baby. You'll also want materials out of which to fashion your own creations. Store your goodies in a shoe bag or covered box. With an eye to the future, keep your box or bag in a convenient place, but out of reach of little groping hands.

Small-Item Storage

A desk organizer drawer insert can be used to separate and organize all those little things, such as pins, swabs, and so on.

Toy Tip

Baby will be the recipient of many thoughtfully chosen toys, although some may be too large, fancy, or advanced for his immediate use. These selections can be attractively displayed if a curtain ring or loop is stitched to the back. Hang these gifts in place of pictures, posters, or other wall decorations until Baby is ready to play with them. They will add appeal and dimension to Baby's room.

Cuddle Along

Let Baby come along when you do a little light housework. Just place him in his front carrier or sling. He will feel cozy and content being close to you, and you will have both hands free to work.

Plan Ahead

By now, there is a pattern to Baby's crying. Like all of us, there are times of the day when Baby is not at his best. Half the battle is discovering these times so that you can plan ahead.

BABY'S BEST

Playtime _____

Eating time _____

Loving time _____

Baby's less than best time _____

_____

Fireproof

Mix—
1 gal. of warm water
9 oz. Borax
4 oz. boric acid solution

To fireproof Baby's bedding and clothing, pour this solution into a bucket in which you can soak all items. Then let the items dry. The protection lasts for from fifteen to twenty washings. You can get the boric acid solution at a pharmacy.

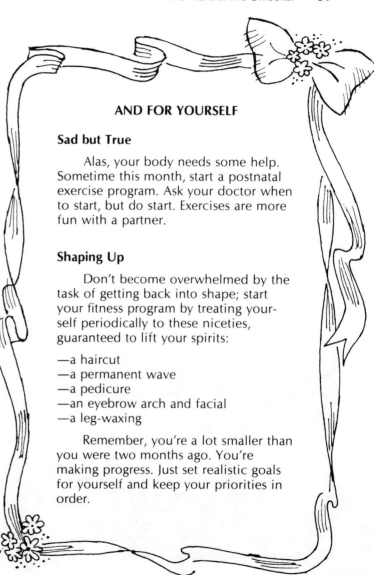

AND FOR YOURSELF

Sad but True

Alas, your body needs some help. Sometime this month, start a postnatal exercise program. Ask your doctor when to start, but do start. Exercises are more fun with a partner.

Shaping Up

Don't become overwhelmed by the task of getting back into shape; start your fitness program by treating yourself periodically to these niceties, guaranteed to lift your spirits:

—a haircut
—a permanent wave
—a pedicure
—an eyebrow arch and facial
—a leg-waxing

Remember, you're a lot smaller than you were two months ago. You're making progress. Just set realistic goals for yourself and keep your priorities in order.

The Real Thing

More visually alert, Baby prefers three-dimensional objects to photographs or drawings.

A Bike Basket

Need an easy-to-install, inexpensive (about $4.00), and attractive catchall? Try a bicycle basket. You can attach several to the end of a standard changing table; or you can mount them on the wall in a convenient place. They come in chrome, wicker, and plastic. Use as is, or spray paint with latex enamel.

Twice Washed

Sensitive skin may react to detergents or special rinses.

To minimize diaper rash or to keep Baby forever free of bumps, wash diapers once with the hottest water and mildest soap. Rinse twice in plain water without rinse additives.

When it comes to drying, the best choice is to hang diapers outside or to tumble dry. Avoid drying on a radiator or over direct heat.

Quickest Dryer

Booties, undershirts, socks, and other small items of clothing will dry quickly in the hood of a hair dryer. You can also direct the airflow from a hand blower toward a garment that has been hung on a rack or hanger to speed the job.

Uniform Measure

Part of the daily uniform is a colorful apron with shoulders and large pockets. These practical garments are essential when living with a young baby, so select several. A durable model made of vinyl can be cleaned with the swish of a sponge.

Nasal Aspirator

A nasal aspirator is a very useful tool when your baby gets a cold. These aspirators, designed for clearing congestion from tiny noses, are available in drugstores. Ask your pharmacist to demonstrate their use and instruct you. Your pharmacist, by the way, is a very knowledgeable resource person.

Some physicians suggest the use of an ear syringe as a nasal aspirator. These syringes fit little noses very well.

Furniture for Adults

The most important pieces of furniture for the adults in the nursery are a cozy rocking chair and a footstool. A sturdy table adjoining the chair to hold items used in feeding or comforting Baby is also handy.

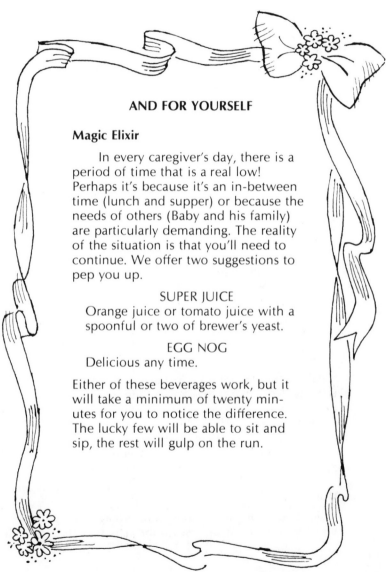

AND FOR YOURSELF

Magic Elixir

In every caregiver's day, there is a period of time that is a real low! Perhaps it's because it's an in-between time (lunch and supper) or because the needs of others (Baby and his family) are particularly demanding. The reality of the situation is that you'll need to continue. We offer two suggestions to pep you up.

SUPER JUICE
Orange juice or tomato juice with a spoonful or two of brewer's yeast.

EGG NOG
Delicious any time.

Either of these beverages work, but it will take a minimum of twenty minutes for you to notice the difference. The lucky few will be able to sit and sip, the rest will gulp on the run.

Things to Try

Many parents report that their infants have fussy periods in the early evening when little seems to help. Here are some remedies that you can try.

—Put Baby in his infant sling or front carrier and go for a short walk.

—Take Baby for a short spin in the car.
—Place Baby in his infant swing.
—Use your trusty rocking chair and sing a lullaby.

All of these suggestions include rhythmic movement, which has been found to have a comforting effect on young infants.

PARENTS, FRIENDS, AND ADMIRERS

Handling

Don't worry about Baby's endurance when it comes to being picked up, moved about, or stimulated. Babies were designed to be handled. One of the ways to truly connect with Baby is to comfort him when he is distressed. This mutual experience, very satisfying to both Baby and admirer, encourages other types of communication.

Waiting

Baby's grandparents are just as close as the telephone. Now that things are settling into a routine, why not call and share with them Baby's latest achievements. These devotees will be delighted to hear every detail of these accomplishments, and your thoughtfulness will be appreciated.

A Must

Do indulge at least once a month in a romantic dinner for two. This is a must for the new parents.

Use candles, wine, flowers, and music. Steak is always a treat; it takes only minutes to fix and is well worth the cost once a month.

Comfort Counts

For the late-night feeder or the caregiver who needs to walk with a light tread, how about a pair of fleece-lined moccasins or a bright pair of down booties? Either choice is unbeatable for cheer and warmth.

Toys

Buy something special for Baby! He has informed us that he loves red and other bright-colored things. Toys must be mouthable. They must have an interesting texture or nooks and crannies for fingers to explore. Please make sure that toys make a noise or have moving parts that won't fall off.

Two-month-olds like teething beads and teething toys. They like soft, rubbery creatures that squeak, mobiles that jump when they do, cradle gyms that have reflecting surfaces and make noises when they finally hit them. Rattles are OK, too.

Ode to Baby

Write your own poem for Baby. Try free verse, rhyme, or even a cinquain, a five-liner. Here is how you do it.

Line 1—one word, title
Line 2—two words, description
Line 3—three words, action
Line 4—four words, feeling
Line 5—one word, a title substitute

For example,
Son
First baby
Experiencing, smiling, wiggling
Such aliveness, such joy
Christopher

YOUR POEM

_____

_____

_____

_____

_____

Men

Given the chance, men can be as sensitive caregivers as women. Research shows that men are more playful and visually attractive to young infants. Learning the features of a variety of loving relationships is very important. One parent or friend does not replace the other. Rather, each adds his or her own unique contributions.

Siblings

Brothers and sisters may be among the first to tell you what they think about Baby. The truth is that Baby cannot play with them, cries a lot (and loudly), receives lots of attention from all the grown-ups, and may not be very cute. There are several things you can do to alleviate the situation.

Special times together without Baby will help relieve anxiety. Brothers and sisters need reassurance that there is enough affection and attention for them, too.

Children under two years of age are probably not going to understand what's happening if they are taken to someone else's home for baby-sitting. It would be easier for the child to remain in his or her own surroundings, even if he or she has to share them.

Three-year-olds and up often find having a baby of their own a way to cope with their mixed feelings. A baby doll with diapers, bottle, bed, and a few pieces of clothing can be used by a child while you deal with Baby's needs.

Schedule

Friends and relatives will want to see Baby, so decide when it's best for both of you. Choose one of Baby's active times so that they can see your bright, alert baby. Introduce them to some of Baby's favorite games.

Thoughtful

Going to visit a friend who just had a baby? Why not take some new fingernail polish and your nail care supplies in a lovely basket. You can trade a manicure for a cup of coffee and help Mom with Baby while her nails are drying.

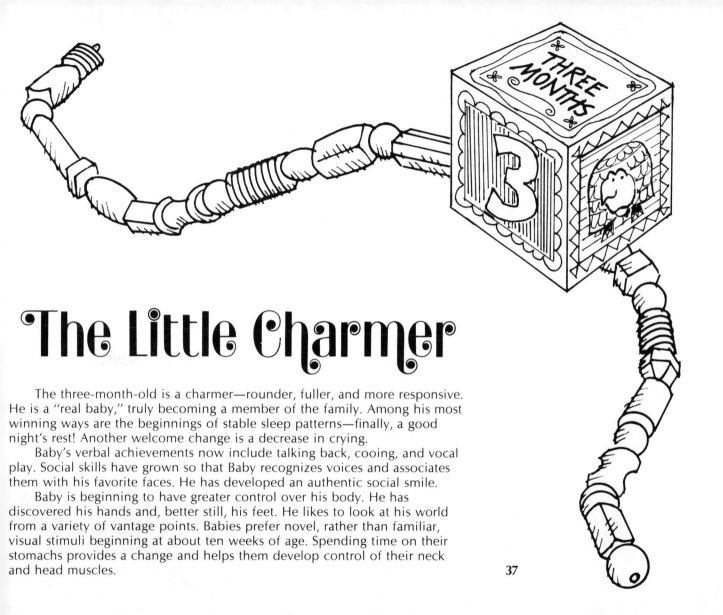

The Little Charmer

The three-month-old is a charmer—rounder, fuller, and more responsive. He is a "real baby," truly becoming a member of the family. Among his most winning ways are the beginnings of stable sleep patterns—finally, a good night's rest! Another welcome change is a decrease in crying.

Baby's verbal achievements now include talking back, cooing, and vocal play. Social skills have grown so that Baby recognizes voices and associates them with his favorite faces. He has developed an authentic social smile.

Baby is beginning to have greater control over his body. He has discovered his hands and, better still, his feet. He likes to look at his world from a variety of vantage points. Babies prefer novel, rather than familiar, visual stimuli beginning at about ten weeks of age. Spending time on their stomachs provides a change and helps them develop control of their neck and head muscles.

37

Though still unable to grasp objects, mobiles and other eye entertainers are an endless source of fascination. They also provide practice for grasping attempts, which resemble a boxer's roundhouse swing. Baby enjoys playing with the rattles placed in his grasp and will retain them. Baby is only able to drop these objects by chance.

Baby strains to sit up and shows his pleasure at being propped up. Whether in a special infant seat, on a lap, or positioned in the corner of the sofa, Baby thrives on being part of the passing scene.

In addition to looking, Baby enjoys listening to music and voices. He uses his voice to attract attention, the first sign of assertive behavior.

ACTIVITIES, GAMES, AND SONGS

A Ball for Baby

Baby might enjoy a small sponge ball. The ball should be tightly textured to withstand constant mouthing.

Timing

Remember that timing is all-important. Playtime will be a "ball" if Baby is well fed, awake, alert, and dry.

Toe Bows

The three-month-old is just discovering that he has toes. A bright red bow on his big toe makes playing with his toes special fun.

Baby makes a swipe for bow but can't quite grasp it

_____

Baby got hold of left bow _____

right bow _____

Oldie but Goodie

Play Peek-a-Boo, still Baby's favorite game. Playing this game is a sure way to see Baby's beautiful smile. There are as many variations to this discovery game as you have time to invent.

To Baby, who does not yet know that things he no longer sees continue to exist, the reappearance of your smiling face is a real surprise.

Easy Listening

Music is a great mood changer, pacesetter, and calming agent, so turn on the record player, tape recorder, or radio. Sing or play an instrument; determine Baby's choices.

BEETHOVEN OR BEATLES

Baby seemed to like:

Record _____

Song _____

Instrument _____

Letting Go

Watch out for bumps. Baby still hasn't quite got the hang of letting go of toys, so save those great wooden toys for later. Lightweight and soft toys are best for now. Baby can accidentally bop himself on the head with the others.

The Mobile

The experts agree that mobiles are "musts" for Baby. They provide color, motion, interest, and incentive for Baby's earliest reaching efforts. The best are mobiles of bright color or shiny features placed within ten to twelve inches of Baby.

Recent studies have suggested that, given the opportunity, babies will learn to control the movement of their mobiles by kicking and squirming, provided that the mobile is attached to the crib in a way that allows this to occur.

One father made instant mobiles with coat hangers and fishing line. He finished his creations with several balls of crumpled aluminum foil.

Tug-of-War

Sew a loop of elastic through a thread spool. Let Baby grasp the spool while you pull gently on the loop. Baby will think this is great fun. Later, these spools can be hung from the crib rail and used for a pulling game that Baby initiates himself.

Talk, Talk, Talk

Baby will now probably begin to recognize your voice by its pitch, volume, and intonation. Include him as you go about your tasks by telling precisely what you're doing—preparing his food, putting on a new striped shirt, getting ready to take a walk, or going to meet new friends. Baby is learning by listening as well as by looking. Give him the opportunity to watch you speak as he listens.

Our Own Game

Our own game together was:

_____

_____

_____

_____

_____

_____

Tracking Practice

Now that Baby's vision allows him to see across the room, he will enjoy games of visual tracking. A flashlight beam on the ceiling or wall is a fun way to lighten a dark room and give Baby's eyes a chance to chase the light.

Cuddle Toys

Baby's earliest companions in the crib, day seat, or on the floor will be a range of furry, soft objects. Check all toys to make certain that decorations cannot be removed by an exploring mouth. The best choices are washable, durable, and make a low sound.

Already there is a favorite toy.

It is a _____

Given by _____

Rattles

This classic toy takes on new meaning as Baby's skills and interests change. Remember that variety is the spice of life. This month a shiny rattle that tinkles has the greatest appeal for Baby.

Tickle Me

Tickle me, tickle me,
Tickle me, whee . . .
Oh, that tickle feels
Good to me.

(Under the chin, on tummy.)

Exercise

Passive exercises were used last month as a way to develop body awareness. They are also a fine way to relax a tense infant. Cycle those legs, rub those arms, pat the tummy, and shake the fingers. If you hum or sing a lullaby, this will aid the relaxation process.

A Name Song

Baby will begin to recognize his own name if you sing it each time you approach him or at special times. Sing to a melody of your choice:

Tell me what your name is.
My name is Grandma (Uncle, Daddy).
I'll tell you what your name is.
Your name is (Lisa).
I'm very glad to see you.

One-Man Band

Colored plastic bangle bracelets make great toys for Baby. Why, with a few bracelets to clang and some bells sewn onto elastic for his ankles, Baby is a one-man band. He will enjoy the music as he kicks and squirms.

Tummy Time

Although Baby may initially resist time on his stomach, this position will give him new sights to see and will also provide practice at raising his head and strengthening his neck. Start slowly—five to ten minutes a day after meals. If you lie down beside him and converse, there will be a real reason for him to raise up and look around.

Rainbow Colors

Buy a package of colored acetate sheets at a school supply store. Cut them into 4 in. x 6 in. panes and sew bias binding around them on your sewing machine.

Tie them onto the crib, between the bars. The light from the window will cast a lovely parade of colors across Baby and his crib.

Yodda-Lay-Dee-Hoo

Listen for those early chortles and gurgles. They are a demand for response. Talk back and Baby will talk, talk, talk. . . . This early imitation game will delight Baby. Someone is finally speaking his language.

Echoes

Baby's responses to my mimicking him were:

_____

_____

_____

_____

_____

Date _____

Kicking Toy

For a change of pace, make a kick toy by hanging a foil pie plate from Baby's mobile. Position it just in reach of his feet or attach the pan to the footboard of the crib. Add bells or a rattle to make successful kicks delightful.

Before you attach the kick toy to the crib, think through how you will attach it. Make sure that Baby cannot catch a foot in the kick toy and become distressed.

Clear-View Envelope

You can make your own clear-view envelope for Baby. Take a piece of heavy, clear vinyl and make a bag or pocket with a finished size of 7 in. x 10 in. Turn back the top edges of the bag 1 in. to form a casing. Now stitch along the edge. Thread two pieces of 36-in. colored ribbon through the casing so that you have two tying ends on each side. Sew or glue velcro tabs or strips along the inside of the opening so the bag can be securely closed.

Stretch the bag across the crib about 12 to 15 inches above Baby's head and tie securely to the crib railings. You can then place all kinds of good things inside for Baby's viewing—a flower, bells, tinsel, pretty fabrics, lollipops, plastic Christmas tree bulbs. Only your imagination will limit you.

Sit Box

By the middle to the end of the third month, you will want a secure way of letting Baby practice sitting for a *short* period of time. Use a small cardboard box, about 9 in. x 12 in. x 9 in. Place Baby in a sitting position in the box. The sides of the box should fit snugly under Baby's arms. Baby's feet should be touching the front of the box. This gives him plenty of support and he can practice sitting without fear of falling. Attach some bells or a toy to the box for Baby to explore.

Move Baby and his box as you go about your daily routines. He will enjoy the companionship and the view, and boredom will not become an issue. This should be only one of many position changes for Baby.

I Wanna See

A curious baby will enjoy observing you doing things for and to him. Mirrors and shiny surfaces hold a special fascination anyway. They never lose their ability to attract Baby's eyes. Mirrors that are mounted so that Baby can see himself are desirable now and later.

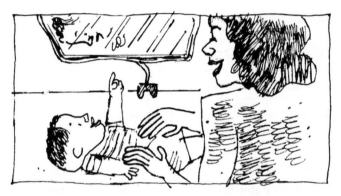

A mirror over the changing table can be reassuring. As Baby gets older, the mirror will be a visual pacifier. Reflective surfaces that will work well as mirror substitutes include sheet aluminum and shiny contact paper. With these, there is no danger of broken glass.

Portrait Gallery

Babies love faces, especially eyes. Favorite faces are those of family and friends, so why not put a gallery of several pictures inside Baby's crib. A clear sheet of contact paper will protect the pictures from exploring hands and tongues later on.

ROUTINE TIMES

Enjoy these daily activities with your very cheerful baby.

BATHING

Three Tips

By now, most babies are accepting the bathing routine. Remember—
1. to add oil to bathwater to keep Baby's skin soft
2. to select an unscented soap to ensure thorough cleansing and protect sensitive skin
3. to always gently pat Baby dry—brisk rubdowns are reserved for adults

Share a Shower

Share water fun with your infant by showering together. A gentle mist or spattering is a welcome surprise, and refreshing, too.

Mothers who have tried this report that their babies were eager, early participants in aquatic programs. Some facilities have courses for infants as young as six months. Call your local YMCA for additional information.

Netted

Use a netlike sack (one that held oranges or potatoes) to hold bath gear—toys, scrubbies, etc. Hang sack over the faucet and allow to dry after bathing.

SLEEPING

Mattresses

Do remember to rotate the mattress in Baby's crib and bassinet. This will increase mattress life and assure more even wear.

Fitted rubber covers that protect the mattress from "accidents" are a must. Quilted mattress pads, which cover these rubber covers, make Baby more comfortable and add to the life of the mattress.

Cover these two items with gay, printed sheets.

Zzzz

Both morning and afternoon naps are more predictable. Baby may sleep two hours in the morning and one and a half in the afternoon.

Baby's schedule is:

_____ A.M. _____ P.M.

_____

_____

_____

_____

_____

(Comments)

Two Are Better

To cover Baby at bedtime, use two or more lightweight blankets rather than just one heavy coverlet. With the multiple blanket approach, there is less bulk, the temperature is easier to regulate, and you have a greater chance of keeping Baby covered. This approach also allows you to wash a blanket at any time and still have a covering for Baby.

Warming Touch

A hot-water bottle takes the edge off cool sheets, enabling Baby to relax and rest. We recently spotted some bottles cleverly concealed as barnyard animals. More like a toy, these bottles were welcomed by a baby we know. These thoroughly washable "pals" can be used to hold ice in case of a bad bump.

FEEDING

A Spoon for Cereal

Most experts recommend that you avoid the shortcut of mixing cereal with milk and putting it into a bottle. If you plan to start solids with Baby, why confuse him? Solids are eaten with a spoon; bottles are for liquids only.

Yum, Yum

By three months, some babies are ready for "real food." They will let you know by showing that they are no longer satisfied with milk. Check with your doctor before adding any new food or beverage to Baby's diet. This decision is strictly between you and your doctor.

Start slowly; a tiny sugar spoon (or demitasse spoon) worth of food each day should be enough. One new food item per week is an easy way to begin.

Don't panic if Baby seems to stop eating altogether. Much is happening—he's learning to swallow, to close his mouth, and to assimilate many new tastes and textures.

Water

Don't forget about plain water. Some babies cry not because they are hungry but because they are thirsty.

Although some nursing mothers advise against ever offering Baby a bottle, more say that getting Baby accustomed to an occasional bottle gives them more freedom in the long run. Don't forget that pumped breast milk can be left in a bottle with a caregiver.

Having a drink of water with Baby is a healthy habit for Mom, too, especially if she is nursing.

Bottle Ready?

By now you can usually anticipate the time of the next feeding. Be prepared, have the gear together and the bottle ready on demand. It is frustrating for a child to have his signal cries for food misunderstood, delayed, or denied. Baby will associate your coming for him at feeding time with the appearance of his bottle.

Blending Ahead

Although Baby may not be ready for solids yet, leftovers can be mashed in a blender or food processor and frozen in ice cube trays. The cubes, each the right size for a meal, will be ready to use in the weeks ahead.

DRESSING AND CHANGING

Favorite Article of Clothing

One of the best ways to dress Baby for fashion and comfort is to join the T-shirt craze. Whether you make your own or purchase souvenir shirts, T-shirts are a welcome change from fussier garments. Brightly colored, inexpensive, usually all cotton, these shirts are fine day or night. Longer shirts can be converted to baby sacques by hemming the bottom and adding a drawstring.

Save outgrown shirts for super toy decorations to make in the months ahead.

Three-Month Poll

Parts of routines Baby has learned to like (or at least accept):

Bathing _____

_____

Sleeping _____

_____

Feeding _____

_____

Dressing and Changing _____

_____

_____

Parts of routines Baby *still* protests (or actively dislikes):

Bathing _____

_____

Sleeping _____

_____

Feeding _____

_____

Dressing and Changing _____

_____

_____

Cold Hands, Warm Heart

Babies frequently have hands and feet that are cold to the touch. Don't consider this a true test of body temperature; the place to check is the tummy. If your home is within a normal temperature range (68° F or above) and Baby has his "work" clothes on (a T-shirt, coveralls or creepers, and diaper), he is probably adequately dressed. If you are concerned about his feet, slip on extra footwear.

HELPFUL HINTS

Reminder

The happy three-month-old baby deserves and delights in more social contact. Let him see and be seen.

Beware of Glare

Babies like soft light from interesting sources. A Mexican tin lantern can provide Baby with a fascinating pattern of light on walls and ceiling.

For a special treat, add a little atmosphere with candlelight while you are with Baby. Baby will be entranced by the flame. Think safety.

Pins and Tape

Keep diaper pins sharp by poking them into a bar of soap when you are not using them.

If you are using disposable diapers, masking tape or plastic tape can be used to replace diaper tape that has been accidentally coated with powder or baby cream.

Perfume or After-Shave

Ah, the sweet, fruity or spicy fragrance of your choice need not wait for a special occasion. The aroma will lift both your spirits and will tantalize Baby's nose. You can spray the air with scent, or sprinkle a bit on the top of a lightbulb to fill the room with interesting smells. You'll find Baby appreciative.

Guilt Fighter

Babies may look frail and helpless, but by the age of three months they do have some toughness. Forgetting to change a diaper occasionally or not doing something right on schedule is not a crisis. Baby will forget and forgive; so, no needless guilts!

Sweet Soakers

Carry a sponge or cloth that has been soaked in a solution of baking soda and water to clean up Baby's bibs and feeding mishaps. Odors will be absorbed quickly.

A Good Night's Sleep

Parents, rejoice! Many infants sleep a continuous ten hours a night by the end of this month. Sleep is guaranteed to make your life easier, so get your rest . . . and thank you, Baby.

Hang Ten

A wall-type hat rack placed close to Baby's changing table will save many steps. Hang washcloths, not-too-soiled undershirts, bibs, etc., on the rack.

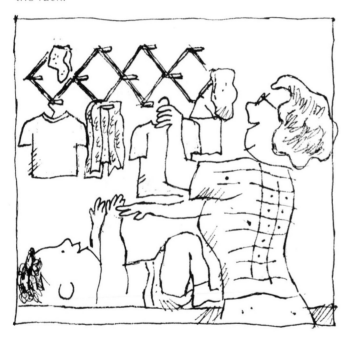

High Polish

To polish the first silver spoon for a tasting baby, try toothpaste. It is absolutely safe, quick, and inexpensive. This works well on rattles and cups, too.

Seat Safety

Now that Baby is becoming more active, never leave him unattended in an infant seat placed on a table or counter. These little seats are tippy, and a sudden jerky movement by Baby could cause an accident.

Sizewise

Planning to make a custom garment for Baby? The only statistics you need for three-month-olds are:

Weight _____

Length _____

These measurements will usually provide a designer with enough information to create a garment that Baby will be able to wear for many weeks. Think comfort and loose-fitting styling. A simple style means quick and easy sewing, and easy laundering, too.

The Entertainer

Baby can keep himself happily occupied for many minutes if there are interesting things to look at in his crib. Give Baby an opportunity for discovery and experimentation, especially in the morning or at the end of a nap. Provide Baby with time and some dangling objects to swipe at or kick. Don't worry, Baby will call you when he needs you.

Fasteners

The fewer snaps, buttons, and zippers on a garment, the easier and speedier dressing will be. Have you heard of velcro? An all-fabric fastener, velcro is tufted nylon material that adheres when pressed to itself. Check it out—strips, tabs, patches, all are great for quick changes.

Bulletin Board

To keep track of supplies, or to record feedings, hang a bulletin board. An invaluable organizer, the bulletin board with pushpins, pen on an attached ribbon, and paper, is a sanity saver.

Diaper Storage

Disposable diapers are cheaper in larger quantities. If you can buy in quantity, an easy way to store a large number is to stack them vertically in a garment bag. The bag can hang, out of sight, in a closet. Besides neatness, you have the advantage of being able to check your supply at a glance.

Place to Go

Remember the library when you need information or inspiration. Whether you need specific answers regarding your child or yourself, it's a quiet and helpful place to spend time.

Fewer Tears

Now is the time when Baby can really accompany you on some small excursions. Most

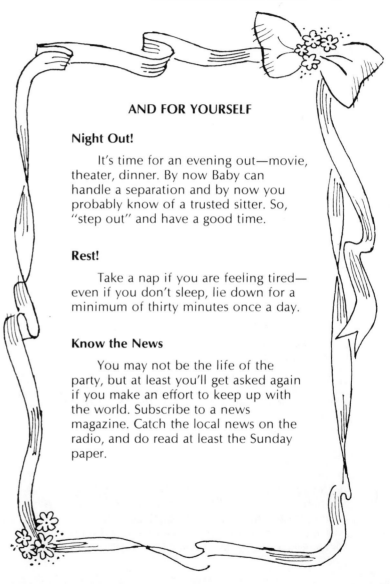

AND FOR YOURSELF

Night Out!

It's time for an evening out—movie, theater, dinner. By now Baby can handle a separation and by now you probably know of a trusted sitter. So, "step out" and have a good time.

Rest!

Take a nap if you are feeling tired—even if you don't sleep, lie down for a minimum of thirty minutes once a day.

Know the News

You may not be the life of the party, but at least you'll get asked again if you make an effort to keep up with the world. Subscribe to a news magazine. Catch the local news on the radio, and do read at least the Sunday paper.

caregivers agree that there is a marked decrease in crying at about three months. If you've only risked a trip to the mailbox until now, it's time to start trying the supermarket, a department store, or even lunch with a friend. Baby can enjoy the view or cuisine from his carriage or infant seat. A change of scene is essential for both you and that smiling, social baby of yours.

Un-stuck

To remove a Band-Aid or adhesive tape from Baby's skin, saturate a cotton ball in baby oil and rub over the tape. No pain, no strain.

Sheets

Making Baby's bed is easy if you use sheets made of stretchy fabric with fitted corners. You can custom design your own model by cutting down a twin sheet. The width of a regular twin is the length of a standard crib. Add elastic in a casing to the corners to keep the new sheet secured and smooth.

A "Must"

To keep you and Baby happy, part of the daily routine should include some time out of the house. Except in the most extreme type of weather, even a short jaunt will do you both good. A change of scene means new things for Baby to see. Other people and stimulating sights can lift your spirits. This planned activity period will minimize the sense of isolation that often occurs when caring for a young child.

Fresh Air

And while you and Baby are out, don't fail to allow Mother Nature an opportunity to contribute to Baby's room. Push back the shutters, open wide the windows, and let the fresh air in to circulate and sweeten. This is by far the fastest and surest way to deodorize a stale room.

PARENTS, FRIENDS, AND ADMIRERS

For "My" Baby

A sibling or other young child will often want to "do" for Baby. Here are a few projects to keep him or her busy.

1. A Cloth Book—pages need be nothing fancier than a few colored fabric swatches. Older children might pink the edges of the pages for a fancy touch. Two holes along one edge laced with a ribbon will hold the book together. Completely washable and visually appealing to Baby, the book can be a crib toy and a gift of love.

2. Young Decorator's Sheets—stretch a portion of a white or solid-colored sheet over an embroidery hoop to hold it steady, then let the child draw, design, or doodle with indelible markers or special fabric crayons. Baby will follow the colors first with his eyes, and later on with his fingers. It's a one-of-a-kind item.

Men

Grandpas, uncles, big brothers, and fathers deserve the thrill of time alone with Baby. Make certain that they know where supplies are located. Post phone numbers and a list of things Baby likes to do. Setting the stage helps ensure success with Baby.

Working Mothers

Here are a few quick thoughts for the mother returning to work.

It is quality time, not quantity time, that counts with Baby.

Baby will always have only one Mommy with whom he shares a very special relationship. Working will never change this. The more you grow as a person, the better mother you will be.

Chitchat

A new face provides a lift for you and Baby. A neighbor child or sibling can entertain and respond to Baby as no adult ever could—just watch! Most older children want very much to really participate in Baby's world, if only anxious parents would let them. Children teach and recognize cues from each other in fresh, spontaneous ways. So disappear and let the "small talk" begin.

Special Folks and Grandparents

Including these not-so-secret admirers in Baby's world is often a challenge. Although proudly possessive, these friends have much to share. Keep them informed by postcard or a quick call if distance separates you; send photos as soon as possible. They are eager to help, so make your suggestions regarding needs, schedules, and routines specific. Showing them in this way that you are on top of the situation will put everyone at ease. These measures will ensure that their efforts will be justly rewarded. Fortunate parents can rely on these people for the best in child care.

BABY VISITED

People	Date

THEY CAME TO SEE BABY

People	Date

Moccasins

If an admirer is traveling to a part of the Old West, a great gift for Baby is a pair of moccasins.

More than a mere novelty, these coverings are an excellent choice for a child who is preparing to crawl. Many are fleece-lined for extra warmth. Soft and flexible, you can make your own from widely available kits.

Remember

What Baby accomplished and how you coped this month will grow difficult to recall all too soon. So take the time now to do some quick jotting.

TIME OUT TO REFLECT ON THE HAPPY MOMENTS
OF THE MONTH

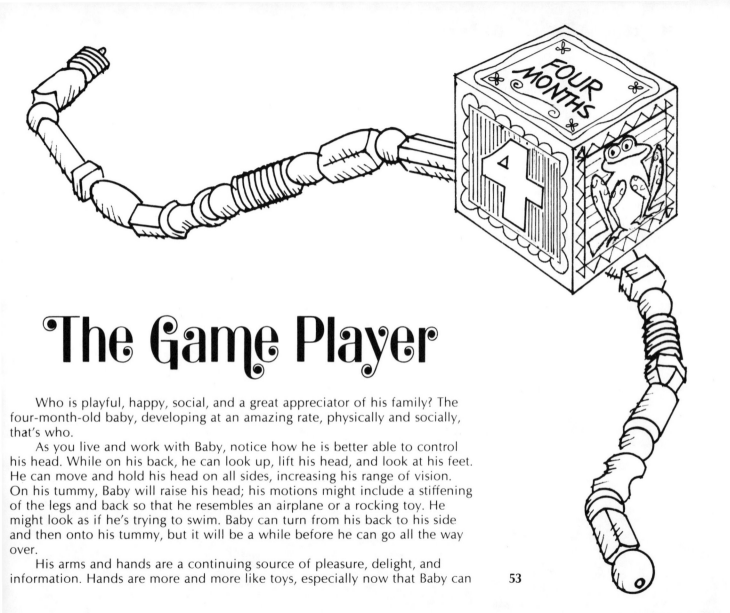

The Game Player

Who is playful, happy, social, and a great appreciator of his family? The four-month-old baby, developing at an amazing rate, physically and socially, that's who.

As you live and work with Baby, notice how he is better able to control his head. While on his back, he can look up, lift his head, and look at his feet. He can move and hold his head on all sides, increasing his range of vision. On his tummy, Baby will raise his head; his motions might include a stiffening of the legs and back so that he resembles an airplane or a rocking toy. He might look as if he's trying to swim. Baby can turn from his back to his side and then onto his tummy, but it will be a while before he can go all the way over.

His arms and hands are a continuing source of pleasure, delight, and information. Hands are more and more like toys, especially now that Baby can bring them together. Little fingers, sensitive to touch, will explore all surfaces, objects, and clothing before bringing whatever possible to Baby's mouth, the taste-tester and first source of information. Arms that are growing strong are being used for pushing up while on his belly and for snaring objects within reach.

Routine times provide opportunities to socialize. Baby wants to talk and to respond to your comments. Just listen for the spontaneous chortles, gurgles, and coos. Bathtime is bliss. Feeding times are the best times of all, but prepare for the mess. This could be a time for fun with father and siblings.

Baby loves to be played with and handled, from casual hugs to gentle roughhousing. Siblings will enjoy this not-so-fragile Baby and can both help out and interact with him easily. Baby's responses will be squeals, smiles, and demands for more. He is a performer, too. Allow him access to a mirror and watch. Baby is a willing participant in any game.

Baby may also grow to prefer a particular toy—one favored above all others. This object may play a special role at rest time, or might help soothe him when he is fussy.

ACTIVITIES, GAMES, AND SONGS

Baby enjoys doing some of his first activities even more now than he did the first time. Do go back and provide lots of opportunities to repeat old favorites.

OUR CHOICES	YOUR CHOICES
1. How Big? (Chapter 1)	_____
	_____
2. Wrist Wear (Chapter 2)	_____
	_____
3. Tracking Practice (Chapter 3)	_____
	_____

Games

Everything you present to Baby is a game. How playful he has suddenly become! If you don't initiate a smile, watch to see if he does. We bet you'll be surprised.

Hot Air

A bunch of brightly colored balloons can be an exciting new toy for Baby. Attach the balloons to his infant seat so they will sway as he moves his body. Keep an eye out for the new foil balloons, too. Their reflection quality is mirror perfect.

Hide-and-Seek

A fun game for an older sibling to play with Baby is hide-and-seek. While Baby is on someone's lap, have a friend call his name and let him turn to find the friend. Baby will enjoy the fun and repetition of this simple game. This is a great activity anytime, especially during routines.

Rolls

Remember the neck-roll pillows your Granny had? These are easy to make and great fun for a young baby getting ready to move. You can place the roll, for short periods of time, under his chest, tummy, or knees, giving his body a new position in space.

A Ball for Baby

Baby will enjoy playing with a multitextured cloth ball or with a molded ball with lots of indentations for exploring fingers.

Changes

As you redecorate, become a collector. A theme approach is just one way to gather posters, prints, and clippings. Try flowers, barnyard animals, food, faces, seasons, wildlife, etc. All your finds can be used for books, puzzles, or games. Remember to cover everything with clear contact paper.

Faces

Use fabric crayons or markers to design the features of an animal or sew a felt face on the top part of Baby's socks. Attach yarn for hair, add buttons, bows, and other finery for a special touch. A fine pair might be a dog and cat, Mom and Dad, or twins. Baby will enjoy watching his feet move and trying to grasp these funny faces.

Body Work

Baby is now really working to know himself—feeling himself, exploring himself and his world. Allow him an opportunity to play alone—perhaps when he awakens in the morning. Such times are learning times; he'll let you know when he wants or needs assistance.

Hands Plus

Because Baby is using his hands more and more, encourage his efforts by giving him a gold star or two. This sparkly reward, stuck onto his wrist, will provide interest for hands and eyes. Place them on other parts of the body, too, perhaps his knee or big toe. Try alternating the stars, red on the top of his wrist, gold for the inside arm. Lately we've spotted piglets, hearts, puppies, and teddy bear gift seals that would also please Baby. If one of these scraps of paper is taste-tested, it will not be a catastrophe.

Dance Partner

A ready partner, should the time be suitable (record, radio, or tape), is Baby. Lift him and waltz, swoop, sway, dip, or jitterbug. Hold each other close and move out onto the dance floor often.

I Can

Baby can, through trial and error, learn to manipulate his own crib gym if he's given the opportunity. Try placing Baby in his infant seat near his gym so that the knobs or things to grasp or hit are suspended just above his lap. He will be delighted with his success. This is the time to include noisemakers, such as a set of metal measuring spoons or jangling plastic bracelets.

Sound Bonanza

Babies learn to listen through practice. "Sound Bonanza" can be a fun game. Put together in a box four or five of Baby's favorite sounds.

OUR LIST	YOUR LIST
Bells	_____
Crinkly paper	_____
Spoons	_____
Squeaker	_____

Play the game by providing Baby with an opportunity to hear each different sound. Start by introducing one or two and slowly include the other sounds until you've presented the entire "Bonanza" to him. Over time you'll notice how Baby learns to anticipate and enjoy this game.

Remember that each room in your house has its own sounds. Baby will grow to associate these sounds and respond to them with recognition and delight.

A Touch of Color

Baby loves his fingers. Examining them is a favorite game. You can add a new dimension with a touch of colored polish on a tiny fingernail.

Rolling Room

Baby can roll now. Make sure to allow room for this activity and give him some incentive. Seeing an item of interest out of the corner of his eye might encourage a roll. For now, these movements may be more like flops, but they are an important stage in his motor development.

Never leave Baby alone on a sofa or bed, no matter how large. Now that he can roll, falls are all too possible.

Mirror Fun

Mirrors are a must for Baby. Use your imagination and place them in places that are accessible to Baby. Nonbreakable mirrors in a variety of shapes and sizes can be purchased at most toy or educational supply stores. Mirrors never lose their intrigue, and can help Baby learn a lot.

Oh Yes, Toes!

Tickle those toes. Remember:

This little Piggy went to market.
This little Piggy stayed home.
This little Piggy had roast beef.
This little Piggy had none.
And this little Piggy cried, "Wee, wee, wee,"
   all the way home.

Fish

Baby loves to watch goldfish. Bright orange and always on the move, they're a real Baby fascinator. A few stalks of fishbowl fern will add additional color and help keep these friends alive.

Be sure to position the bowl close enough to Baby's crib for "live entertainment." But the bowl must be far enough away so that someday soon Baby won't surprise you with a fish in his hand and water all over his crib.

Horsie, Horsie

To the tune of "Here We Go 'Round the Mulberry Bush," sing the following verse as you gently bounce Baby on your knee.

This is the way the lady rides,
  the lady rides, the lady rides.
This is the way the lady rides,
  when she goes into town.
This is the way the gentleman rides . . .
  when he goes into town.
This is the way the farmer rides . . .
This is the way the hunter rides . . .
This is the way the Indian rides . . .

Watch Baby's behavior; see how he shows that he wants you to continue the game. Men seem to be especially good at this game.

Children's Records

Children's records that include action songs can be a good investment. Buy a sturdy child's record player, one an elementary schoolchild can learn to operate. Baby will enjoy listening to the records now. He will try to do the actions with you as a toddler, and sing along as a preschooler. Children like to hear the same several songs many times and are just getting the hang of things about the time adults are ready to scream, so do plan to listen a lot to the ones you choose. Remember that a lot of learning takes place through the medium of music.

Lower, Please

Baby is no longer happy simply watching toys sway before his eyes. He may even wail in frustration. He wants to touch and inspect now. Lower the crib gyms and sturdy, safe mobiles so that they are within easy reach of Baby. He will enjoy practicing this new game of eye-hand coordination. He will diligently work, adjusting his aim until he is finally able to touch and hold these tantalizing toys.

Other Babies

An exciting experience for Baby will be meeting and watching his first other baby. It will be fun for you, too. You will be amazed at the two babies' instant awareness of and interest in each other. Lay the two infants side by side on a blanket where they can truly investigate each other. It would be fascinating to know just what they are thinking.

ROUTINE TIMES

BATHING

Splashes

Happy splashes will be part of bathtime for both of you by now. Remember to wear an apron (oilcloth or vinyl) if you don't want to be dampened. A nice addition to the bath might be a drop or two of food coloring. Don't use too much, or you'll have a strawberry or blueberry baby.

Body Wise

Naming parts of Baby's body is a good thing to remember at bathtime. Start at the head and work down, giving an order to this body awareness routine. Telling him what is being done as you proceed is very reassuring. "I am now washing your arm, your hand . . . give me your other foot . . ." In time, Baby will learn to respond by presenting the appropriate part for a scrub.

Water Play

Baby is not too young for water play. He will enjoy paddling hands and feet in warm water. For the reluctant bather, this mini-experience might be a help in learning to cope with a larger tub.

Bath Toy

A fluffy nylon net flower makes a tickly bath toy. You can often buy these at local bazaars or craft outlets.

Best Bath

Baby likes his bath best after his meals, when he is full, relaxed, and happy. Often this will be the time when he needs one. Experience will quickly teach you when not to bathe Baby; for example, when he is overtired or hungry.

Rub-a-Dub-Dub

An open-weave plastic laundry basket is a safe way to secure Baby in a tub. Run an inch or two of water in the tub and watch him enjoy his new environment. This is also a great way to have fun outside with water; use a small inflatable pool.

SLEEPING

Sleep Time?

Baby is growing quite comfortable in his bedtime routine. Make sure that stability continues by sticking to the same bedtime with as few exceptions as possible. Put him down in the way he prefers, with or without favorite toys. Make him cozy, sing, say goodnight, and leave calmly.

Baby on the Go

It is important that parents be aware of Baby's napping routine, even if Baby spends most naptimes away from home. By providing some continuity, weekends can be more enjoyable. Having a bedfellow who comes and goes with Baby can be helpful. So is knowing whether Baby naps in a quiet room or if his crib remains in a lighted room where other children are playing. Good communication among Baby's favorite people benefits all.

FEEDING

By now Baby probably no longer requires a late night feeding. During the day, he is steadily eating every three to four hours. Since Baby is beginning to try "people food," you might consider:

—bananas in thin slices
—a toast finger
—a graham cracker
—a popped pea or two (a pea that has been poked by a fork)
—a tablespoonful of applesauce

Baby's Treat Sheet

ITEM PRESENTED   DATE   REACTION

_____

_____

_____

_____

_____

Food Facts

Keep food simple; no combinations, please. By presenting a single serving, food intolerance can be immediately detected. When Baby wants to be fed again, he will let you know.

A handy way to keep a variety of food for Baby is to use a plastic popsicle kit. A few tablespoonfuls of fruit or vegetable easily fit into each well. Cap to preserve flavor and taste.

Remember that your homemade concoctions should not be kept longer than three days. If you have any doubts, throw it out.

Bib

Playing with food is nearly as interesting as eating to Baby. So make a couple of quick bibs; use washcloths or kitchen towels, 13 in. x 10½ in. These will help keep Baby clean and covered. Cut a half circle for the neck, bind edges with bias tape, and stitch long lengths for ties.

DRESSING AND CHANGING

Jingle-Bell Jack

A nifty shirt is one that has several things going for it. Baby and Mom like it to be easy to get into, washable, and an unexpectedly brilliant color. You could make a surprise shirt by sewing on a bell or a noisemaker. Attach the item securely or conceal it artistically so that it is worn, not swallowed. Baby and Mom will love it.

Bells and noisemakers are also great additions to shoes or booties.

Clothes Horse

Looking at those adorable clothes that no longer fit is discouraging, so may we suggest:
1. Cutting the sleeves out of shirts for that "muscle beach" or layered look
2. Stuffing old socks and booties for a soft sculpture or mobile
3. Saving the best and favorite items for Baby's larger stuffed friends and dolls to wear

4. Swapping with a friend whose children are older *and* younger than Baby

The Strap

Your little wiggler, in a fit of temper, could launch himself right off a changing table. For security, both yours and his, remember the strap. A midriff belt will do the trick.

Flat Out

If you are caught off guard by the telephone, doorbell, or some emergency, and you need free hands or arms, remember that the floor is the best place for an infant halfway between being diapered and dressed.

Diaper Rash

Some suggestions:
1. For an easy and often successful treatment, lay a large plastic tablecloth on the floor and cover with a sheet or mattress pad that can be laundered easily. Allow a diaperless baby to play there with his toys for at least thirty minutes, giving the affected area time to thoroughly dry in the warm room air. If routinely done several times a day for three to five days, this treatment can promote healing. This can also be used as a preventive measure.
2. Rubber pants are often the culprit. Use them only when really needed because they limit the circulation of air around Baby's bottom.
3. Cornstarch works as well as talcum powder in a pinch.

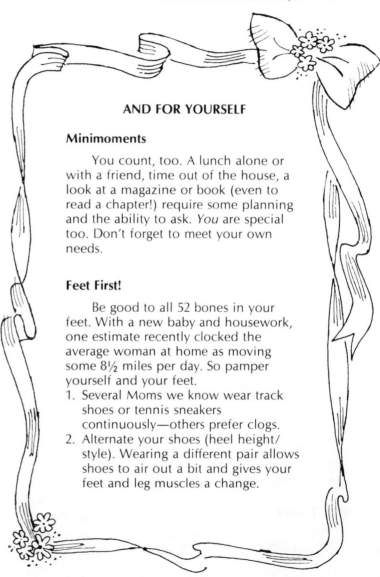

AND FOR YOURSELF

Minimoments

You count, too. A lunch alone or with a friend, time out of the house, a look at a magazine or book (even to read a chapter!) require some planning and the ability to ask. *You* are special too. Don't forget to meet your own needs.

Feet First!

Be good to all 52 bones in your feet. With a new baby and housework, one estimate recently clocked the average woman at home as moving some 8½ miles per day. So pamper yourself and your feet.
1. Several Moms we know wear track shoes or tennis sneakers continuously—others prefer clogs.
2. Alternate your shoes (heel height/ style). Wearing a different pair allows shoes to air out a bit and gives your feet and leg muscles a change.

HELPFUL HINTS

Reminder

We will bet that if you are bored, Baby is too. Think for two; plan ahead. The smallest changes make the hour, morning, or day a special one.

Rested

Have you noticed that things are getting easier? Everyone, including Baby, is getting more rest. Certain routines are becoming established. Baby is more predictable and you can plan the best times to play with him.

Sit Box

Keep your sit box (see Chapter 3, "Activities, Games, and Songs") for a safe alternative to Baby's infant seat. Great to have handy when you travel or must make a quick trip to the second floor. Try covering it with washable, printed contact paper.

Beach Blanket Bingo

Since Baby will be spending more time on the floor, change his surroundings by putting him down on a large, colorful beach blanket or bath sheet. The texture will amuse him and so will the design. This is especially handy when visiting friends.

Last Diaper

Tired of reaching into a box or drawer of diapers only to find that someone has used the last one? Buy a wicker wine rack and stack diapers (cloth or disposable) in the handy sections. This attractive and orderly way of storing diapers lets you see how many are left. After Baby's diaper days are over, you can move this storage item to the pantry and use it for its intended purpose.

Sniff-less

Two deodorizers for the refrigerator, now full of odd baby food concoctions, are:
1. A box of baking soda
2. A chunk of charcoal

Both items will absorb odors and keep foods tasting the way they were meant to taste.

Medical Note

By now Baby should be halfway through his immunization program. Completion of this program ensures a healthy baby. Check to make sure things are on schedule; keep a record at home.

Heloise?

My Helpful Hint for Heloise this month would

be: _____

_____

_____

Your Observer

Baby wants to see you doing things. The most common household task is still new to him. Companionship is part of what Baby is after. He also loves an opportunity to chatter with you. So move him with you in his sit box, sling, high chair, or swing, or make a place for him on the floor. Make sure he is positioned so that he has a good view of the action and that you are not far away.

The Packed Baby

One way to make the quick trip a more frequent happening is to have an extra bag of gear ready to go. Just like an overnight bag that can be grabbed for a dash to the airport, prepare so that you and Baby can leave with a minimum of fuss.

Include

—diapers (disposable/cloth)
—powders or cream (sample size)
—a complete change of clothes
—a sweater
—a blanket
—disposable wet paper towels

Repack your bag after each trip and you'll be ready for next time.

Stroller Tips

Storage tips for your umbrella stroller—the greatest invention since disposable diapers—include

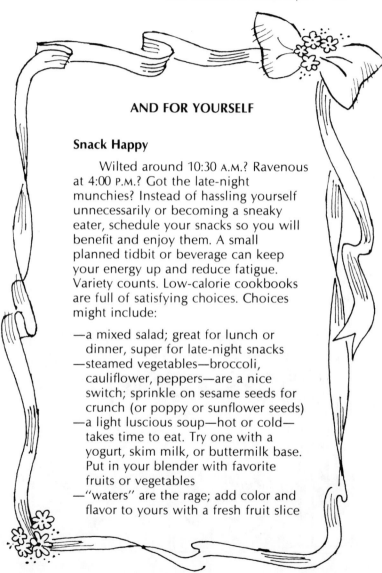

AND FOR YOURSELF

Snack Happy

Wilted around 10:30 A.M.? Ravenous at 4:00 P.M.? Got the late-night munchies? Instead of hassling yourself unnecessarily or becoming a sneaky eater, schedule your snacks so you will benefit and enjoy them. A small planned tidbit or beverage can keep your energy up and reduce fatigue. Variety counts. Low-calorie cookbooks are full of satisfying choices. Choices might include:

—a mixed salad; great for lunch or dinner, super for late-night snacks
—steamed vegetables—broccoli, cauliflower, peppers—are a nice switch; sprinkle on sesame seeds for crunch (or poppy or sunflower seeds)
—a light luscious soup—hot or cold—takes time to eat. Try one with a yogurt, skim milk, or buttermilk base. Put in your blender with favorite fruits or vegetables
—"waters" are the rage; add color and flavor to yours with a fresh fruit slice

—hanging it on an old-fashioned clothes hook
—setting it in an old wicker umbrella holder or tall wicker basket
—storing it in a bottom bureau drawer

Lickety-Split

A baby front-carrier can be turned into an emergency high chair for Baby by placing him in the sling and tying it to a chair. This will give Baby's back needed support. It also provides an element of safety in that he is securely tied to the chair. It can be handy when you are at a friend's home and want to have your arms free to sip your coffee. It also allows your social baby to stay close to your side.

"Two in One" Bag

It's worth the effort and time to develop a "two-in-one" bag to take Baby and his belongings to day care or the baby-sitter. Ideally the bag should allow for the large section of the bag to remain during the week. The small bag should be detachable so that soiled clothes can be taken home daily. It can also be used to transport daily food and needed extras.

Pop-Tops

A "fashion" poncho can provide quick coverage for a busy Baby. These easy pop-tops can be made for rain, sun, or cool temperatures at the beach or in the backyard.

1. The Raintop can be made of lightweight vinyl or a similar fabric. No hemming required; just bind neck edge with ribbon or seam binding.
2. The Suntop, a cool, absorbent cover to keep the ultraviolet rays away from sensitive skin, can be made from an extra hand towel, standard size. A fringe front and back adds a festive look.
3. For cooler days—an extra blanket from Baby's collection will make a fine washable cover.

PARENTS, FRIENDS, AND ADMIRERS

Special Toy

A simple rag doll or a monkey made of socks is a good choice for Baby this month. Soft enough to gnaw on without teeth, durable, and cuddly, these toys are easily made at home. Patterns and kits are readily available. Or, make up your own little creatures from your scrap bag.

Brothers and Sisters

Baby is becoming more responsive and no one is more delighted than his siblings. Baby can do more and is less apt to cry when bumped, startled, or loved by his family. Rivalries will at last be under control.

Sound Machine

The most patient interpreters of your little noise machine are probably grandparents. These admirers, long on experience, will be best able to imitate and initiate Baby's sounds. Watch them, and pick up some valuable techniques.

Young Art

Baby will enjoy the colorful art of brothers, sisters, or young neighborhood friends. He especially likes faces that can be dangled for his amusement or used to brighten his room.

Frame especially nice artwork from Baby's siblings and hang in his room. This is a good way to flatter the brother or sister who may need a pat on the back just about now.

Sprouting

Baby is growing fast.

Current length _____

Current weight _____

Favorite Toys _____

_____

_____

An Early Start

Now that Baby is four months old it's time for friends and admirers to think about his future. A piggy bank may be corny and old-fashioned, but it's a nice way to start thinking ahead for this special baby.

Notes for Special Host/Hostess

Here are some suggestions that should make Baby's stay with a special admirer especially fun. Prepare now and have these items close at hand.

—This book, so you will know Baby's favorite games
—Some well-chosen toys
—A cozy, safe place to sleep
—A familiar toy and blanket from home

Instant Bed

The floor is a perfect place for a visiting baby. Place a plastic mat from a playpen or an air mattress on the floor, cover with an old quilt or blanket, and partition off a cozy space with pillows. This will provide a safe place for this little wriggler to sleep in comfort.

Napping Hints

Techniques you might use when napping your visiting baby are:

—Lay Baby down, dim the lights, turn on the radio very softly, and creep out. Wait about five minutes to see if he falls asleep.
—Rock and walk Baby until he starts to fall asleep, then lay him down.
—Pat or rub Baby's back as he lies on his tummy in bed until he quiets and slips off to sleep.

Voices

Baby will respond to a new voice. Notice how alert he becomes when a visitor or stranger appears. It is one of many ways Baby learns about people in his world. Give him exposure to new voices.

Fathers

Dads and other involved men play a continuing role in Baby's development. These important people communicate with Baby their special way of handling, care, and concern. Their body language is picked up in ways that many babies respond to positively and with delight. Men are great caregivers and can change, bathe, and feed successfully.

Personality Chart

Baby has a very definite personality and temperament. Take time to jot down a few notes about Baby's emerging style.

_____

_____

_____

_____

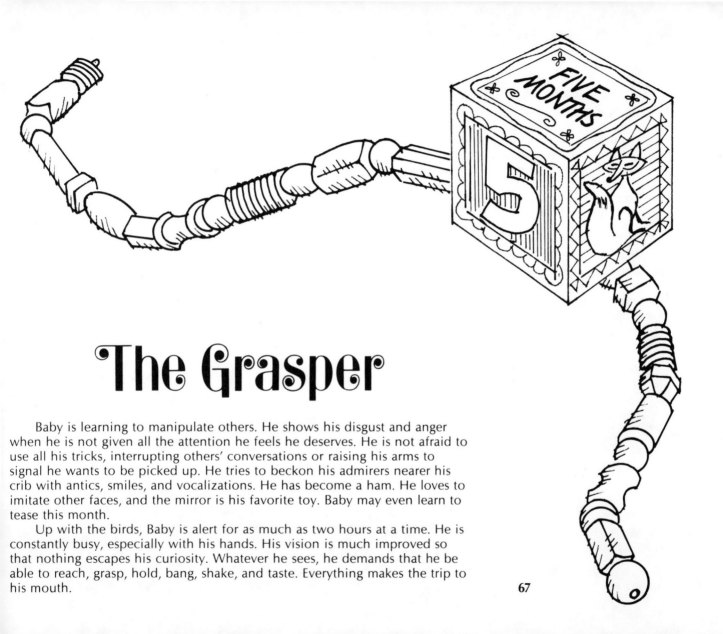

The Grasper

Baby is learning to manipulate others. He shows his disgust and anger when he is not given all the attention he feels he deserves. He is not afraid to use all his tricks, interrupting others' conversations or raising his arms to signal he wants to be picked up. He tries to beckon his admirers nearer his crib with antics, smiles, and vocalizations. He has become a ham. He loves to imitate other faces, and the mirror is his favorite toy. Baby may even learn to tease this month.

Up with the birds, Baby is alert for as much as two hours at a time. He is constantly busy, especially with his hands. His vision is much improved so that nothing escapes his curiosity. Whatever he sees, he demands that he be able to reach, grasp, hold, bang, shake, and taste. Everything makes the trip to his mouth.

He now looks after fallen objects and recognizes familiar objects. He is developing a memory and remembers some of his own actions. With his good vision, he can now recognize members of his family and may bounce and wiggle with delight when he spots them approaching. By the same token, he is likely to be more wary of strangers.

Baby is beginning to understand language. He knows his name and babbles to gain attention. He enjoys experimenting with sounds and inflection patterns, trying to imitate what he hears. He vocalizes to himself, his toys, and his admirers. He watches mouths very carefully, sharpening his skills.

Motor skills may be developing rapidly. On his tummy, he lifts his head chest-high off the bed as he bounces and wiggles. He is beginning to locomote by rocking, rolling, twisting, or pushing against flat surfaces. He can sit supported for thirty minutes. He likes to stand when supported and will sway, stomping his feet. Remember, however, that babies are individuals; not all will develop this rapidly.

Baby is leaving the quiet months of looking and is about to become very mobile, someone from whom nothing is safe. This is the time for parents and others who have infants in their homes to begin babyproofing.

ACTIVITIES, GAMES, AND SONGS

Swinging Eggs

An inexpensive crib gym for Baby can be made from metallic egg-shaped panty hose containers. Simply add rice, beans, or bells, a string, and seal the eggs tightly. These can then be dangled from a piece of elastic stretched across the crib. Babies love shiny objects, and will enjoy hearing them jingle and trying to catch them as they sway.

Bubbles

Babies love bubbles and will sit spellbound watching you blow them. Make your own mix using ½ cup dishwashing liquid, a tablespoon of glycerine, and a small amount of water. A straw or the frames from an old pair of sunglasses will make the perfect blower or wand. If time is money, buy a jar of bubbles at the dimestore. They are still inexpensive and a very good buy.

Surprise

Hide a squeak toy under Baby's sheet or blanket. Show Baby how to squeak it with his hand. Soon, with a little practice, he'll learn to squeak it himself. For an additional surprise, hide a squeak toy in the pocket of Baby's coat or in the jacket of a friend.

Puzzles

It's not too soon for knob puzzles (puzzles with little knobs on each piece for easy lifting and holding). Babies enjoy looking at them, chewing on them, and distinguishing their colors and shapes. Add knobs of your own to wooden puzzles. It's difficult to lose pieces with these quick-to-attach handles.

Music

Music is a language of its own, one that Baby can enjoy and understand. A nice way to start a nap might be with a little soft classical music. Playtime can include lively music to sway to. Watch Baby's reactions.

Musical Instruments

Baby will enjoy making music with bells. In Chapter 3 he had an anklet with bells. This month he will be able to grasp some bells joined together. Another fine choice would be a pair of maracas for him to shake.

Handles

Toys with handles will be special fun this month. A stuffed chick with wings to hang onto or a friend with a tail would be great; so would an octopus, monkey, rhino, or elephant. Pick durable and washable toys.

A Left Hook

Waiting in a high chair can be more bearable for Baby if you place a few toys with vacuum-cup bases on his tray. These inexpensive items are fun to hit and they will stand still for a swinging baby. One child we know liked a little bear, circle of balls, and several small animals. Most of these toys will jingle or make a noise when poked or squeezed.

Slick and Shiny

Stuffed oilcloth shapes with bells and rattles inside are welcome new toys. Since Baby is involved with carrying around, holding, and mouthing objects, these washable playthings are practical, too. The fabric itself can determine the final shape. A cheery vinyl pattern with luscious oranges, grapes, and cherries inspired a fruit basket of goodies stuffed with foam rubber. The fruits were also perfect for bathtime toys.

Fire trucks, apples, and hearts drawn freehand, cut from red oilcloth, and stuffed with polyester batting give Baby a slick and shiny surface that will tickle his tongue. A quick sponging or immersion in soapy water and the toys will look great again.

A Ball for Baby

Try stringing three or four table tennis balls on a fishing line. Baby will enjoy grasping and shaking them. In the months to come, they will be fun for the crawling Baby to roll and chase.

Knots

Play teaches Baby about himself and his world. An intriguing toy for Baby this month is a one-inch-thick cotton cord with knots tied at intervals. This simple string toy—approximately six inches long—satisfies Baby's desire to touch and explore.

Making Faces

Baby loves to imitate your funny faces. He will also try to imitate your voice inflections, so use lots of them. See how Baby watches your mouth and then experiments.

Imitator's Notebook

Describe below some of Baby's best imitations of friends and family members.

_____

_____

_____

_____

Pat-a-Cake

A hand-clapping game for you and Baby is:

Pat-a-cake, pat-a-cake,
Baker's man;
Bake me a cake
As fast as you can.
Roll it and pat it
and mark it with B,
And put it in the oven
For Baby and me.

Custom T-shirt

A T-shirt for Baby, one that will be fun for you both, is one that includes a detachable toy. How about a sunny breakfast shirt with snap-on eggs (fried, of course) and bacon strips. Or a fluffy mama cat with a kitten attached with velcro strips.

Produce Exploration

An unlikely but fascinating source of items for exploration is as near as the fruit basket or vegetable bin. Baby will examine, in the greatest detail, texture, shape, and aroma when a basket of these goodies is placed in front of him. Excellent choices include a stalk of leafy celery, a shiny purple eggplant, a fuzzy peach, a slick onion, and a pungent orange. If Baby actually manages to pick anything up, his toothless attempts to gnaw can do little actual harm to these pieces of produce.

Changing Terrain

Lifting one end of Baby's bed can create a new dimension in his environment. He will enjoy this new hill and slide on which to climb and roll. For safety's sake, do this only when you can be present to supervise.

Sing

Sing "Pop Goes the Weasel"—bring Baby's hands together to make the popping sound or clap your hands. Within a few months, Baby will be clapping hands on his own.

All around the cobbler's bench
The monkey chased the weasel.
The monkey thought 'twas all in fun
Pop . . . goes the weasel.

Just Out of Reach

Baby will be working hard this month to make his body move. His rocking, wiggling, arching, and rolling may eventually lead him to crawl. Encourage him to move forward by positioning toys and attractive objects just beyond his grasp. To help a noncrawling baby give the technique a try, sit with the toys yourself an arm's length away to persuade him to move his body.

Inner Tube

A favorite toy is a black rubber inner tube. It is great fun to sit in, pat, and poke. It adds the security of a bit of extra support for the beginning sitter and provides a challenging embankment to scale for the very active baby.

Inner tubes are still easy to come by; check your local tire store or service station. During the summer months, inner tubes of brightly colored lightweight plastic are often sold as beach toys.

Just Like Me

Now that Baby enjoys imitating motions, you can help him develop these gestures into a game. Pick actions that Baby can do spontaneously. Sing as you do them together. For example:

Pat, pat, pat the table,
Pat, pat, pat the table,
Just like me.

As you play, Baby will get the idea and follow along. This is also a good learning experience. Baby hears the words as you do the actions. Other actions might include pull your toe, touch your head, pat your tummy, etc.

ROUTINE TIMES

BATHING

Shampoo Tips

Dealing with Baby's fuzz or first hair can be accomplished if shampoo or bath soap is applied first to a washcloth and then to the head. Baby shampoo is gentle and seems not to bother infants' eyes.

Best Water Toy

Your sitting baby is beginning to play gleefully at bathtime. And you are relaxed and enjoying this ritual more, too.

A few simple bath toys can add to the experience. Besides a cup and sponge, several table tennis balls will add new interest. These lively balls will float and bob for Baby. With a permanent laundry marker, draw happy faces on the balls or decorate them with a stripe or two.

For a jellyfish, just draw a face on one of the balls with an indelible laundry marker and cover with an 8 in. x 8 in. square of nylon netting. Secure with a rubber band. These bobbing jellyfish make nice soft scrubbers for dirty knees, and they are great bath toys.

Jingle, Jingle

Add a jingle to bathtime. Make washcloths easy to locate by sewing a bell onto the corner of a terry cloth washrag.

SLEEPING

Five More Minutes

Now that Baby is rising at dawn, you may be able to grab a few more minutes of sleep by making sure his crib is an interesting place. Put a full array of toys, including his special friend, in Baby's crib at bedtime. Most babies are willing to play happily alone if they don't realize that you are awake. Stay in bed until you hear his loudest protests.

Crib Time

Baby is quickly approaching the size and age when the only truly safe sleeping place is his full-size crib. Time to put away the cradle or bassinet and to limit the use of the pram to strolling.

FEEDING

Eating and Feeding

Baby is all action where food is concerned. Messy times are to be expected. Baby's way of tasting includes lip licking, fist smearing, face painting with food, and inserting utensils and fingers into dishes for just one more taste. It's apron time for you. A cheery apron of wipe-off vinyl or very washable cotton can help you enjoy these antics. An old shower curtain, drop cloth, plastic tablecloth, or plastic sheet will minimize cleanup.

Bottle Sensation

A cover for his slippery bottle is a pleasure for Baby. A colorful sock makes gripping his own bottle easier and provides a tactile experience. A terry cloth handle cover, one designed for a tennis racket, makes a quick cover and helps identify his bottle at day care.

Slip a cover you've made from flannel or stretchy knit material over the bottle and Baby will have something that will help him keep the bottle within his grasp.

The Teether

Got a drooling or grumpy baby? Is he playing with or banging his head? It may not be an earache, but rather the emergence of a new tooth. A teething goody would probably help. See Chapter 7 for "Teething Tips" and "Grandma's Teething Biscuits."

Before Dinner

Keep a busy, hungry baby occupied while you prepare his meal by handing him his own special sponge. Just for the sheer joy of patting, poking, punching, and gumming there are few toys that compare to a dampened sponge. Pick the brightest, most durable one you can find.

Disaster-Day Cooking

On a day that ends as if a national emergency had struck, or on one when cooking for anyone is a low priority, keep an emergency kit containing Baby's favorite foods, ones that need no cooking, in the pantry or refrigerator to see him through mealtime.

Some things to have on hand:

—applesauce
—baby cereal
—yogurt
—a few jars of commercial baby food

Routine Times

The Cup—it's time to master something new! Babies seem to prefer a sturdy cup: a plastic, two-handled, weighted model is a fine beginning. Expect little nourishment to actually reach Baby. These first attempts at drinking will be truly experimental. Remember to use the nonspill drinking lid that comes with the cup while Baby experiments with upside down.

Beauty Parlor Trick

Slipping several tissues, a soft paper napkin, or some toilet tissue around Baby's neck before you put on his bib can make cleanup easier. Learning to eat solids is a messy task. It seems much of his meal becomes liquid feed and rolls down his chin and neck. Using this borrowed idea will keep Baby comfortable and his clothes dry.

DRESSING AND CHANGING

Dressing

Babies are often irritated by fabrics, wool and plastic in particular. They often react to the ties on bibs. Clip the strings and add

—preshrunk grosgrain ribbon
—cloth strips
—bias tape
—two clothespins and a length of string

Diapering Safety

Do, do, do use your safety strap on the changing table. You no longer have a little stay-put baby. Don't, don't ever turn your back on this wiggler, even with his safety strap fastened.

Diaper Liners

A diaper liner is a very handy item to use with cloth diapers; many mothers swear by it. Made of soft cloth, like paper, it fits between Baby and his diaper. It makes cleanup easier and keeps diapers from becoming as heavily soiled. These liners are quite inexpensive.

Size Chart

Shirt size _____

Suit size _____

Weight _____

Length _____

Jot these measurements down and refer to them when you shop for Baby.

Favorites

Baby's favorite sleepmates:

_____

_____

Favorite foods:

_____

_____

Favorite toys:

_____

_____

Favorite games:

_____

_____

Favorite song/music:

_____

_____

Best way to make baby smile:

_____

_____

Baby's current achievements:

_____

_____

HELPFUL HINTS

Reminder

When planning for play, think safety first. Then, make sure there are a lot of opportunities for practice in babyproofed surroundings.

Relaxing

If Baby wants to sit alone but still needs a little support, consider letting him use a pillow with a back and arms like those used for reading in bed. This will provide three-way safety for an easily toppled infant.

Baby Fun

A fun game for Baby, one that is often no fun for busy friends, is "Watch the Toy Fall." Use short elastic bands to attach several toys to his high chair; this can be a backsaver. Baby is not yet able to retrieve his own toys, but this will make the job easier for you.

Remodeling

It's time for a change of environment for Baby. Take down the remaining eye-only tantalizers and bring out the made to touch, taste, wave, and bang ones. Baby is at a stage where he is frustrated by eye-only things. He's into touching in a big way!

Busy boxes and mouthable, soft rubber toys will catch Baby's attention. A selection of wooden spoons of different shapes and sizes makes an inexpensive toy that he will enjoy. Plan Baby's environment to include safe crib toys he can play with while the family gets a few extra winks.

Extra Towel

Sometimes you need just one extra towel and don't want to make a serious job out of hanging it. A plastic suction cup with hooks will hold a light cloth wherever it will serve you best. These cups can be bought at hardware stores or bath shops.

Vanity

Mirrors are still pleasing. A quick way to handle a crying baby is to take him to a mirror. He is so pleased with himself that a sneaky peek will convince him to quiet down and show his better self.

Group Care

Feeding more than one baby at a time? You can heat several bottles at once in an electric bottle sterilizer. These appliances, which hold from six to eight bottles at one time, can be left running throughout the day. They need only a little water added periodically. This is how day-care centers do it.

Milk Stains

To remove milk stains, soak in cold water for about fifteen minutes. Hot water will set milk stains.

Babyproof Now

Start changing your habits now, before it's absolutely necessary. Evaluate everything you do. For example, start now to turn all pot handles in when cooking on the stove. Return all caps and lids to bottles immediately, and give them an extra turn. Sweep often to remove all dangers from Baby's favorite play surface, the floor.

Outlet Covers

For electrical cords you cannot remove from their sockets, there are socket protectors that fit over the sockets and plugs; this makes them safe for Baby. These protectors are also handy for items you do not wish to unplug, such as lamps, stereo, and TV. You'll be glad you have done this when Baby surprises you by reaching for the socket.

Coverage

When visitors come to call, do not hesitate to offer them a diaper, towel, or lap pad along with Baby. This measure is essential if Baby is to be invited back to the visitor's lap.

Softeners

Most mothers are very careful about the soaps they choose for laundering their infants' clothing, but they may not pay equal attention to their choice of fabric softeners. Many softeners that are fine for the family's clothes can irritate Baby's delicate skin. If your child has a problem rash, consider these softeners as possible culprits.

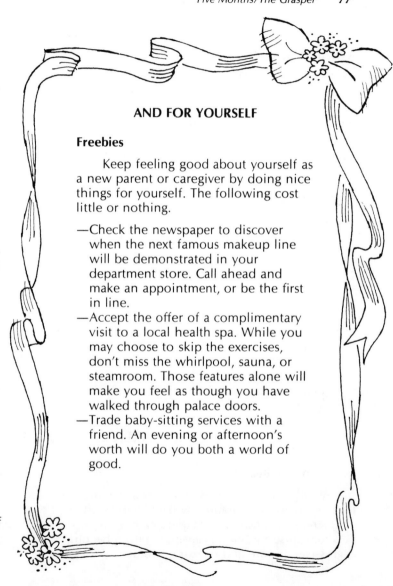

AND FOR YOURSELF

Freebies

Keep feeling good about yourself as a new parent or caregiver by doing nice things for yourself. The following cost little or nothing.

—Check the newspaper to discover when the next famous makeup line will be demonstrated in your department store. Call ahead and make an appointment, or be the first in line.

—Accept the offer of a complimentary visit to a local health spa. While you may choose to skip the exercises, don't miss the whirlpool, sauna, or steamroom. Those features alone will make you feel as though you have walked through palace doors.

—Trade baby-sitting services with a friend. An evening or afternoon's worth will do you both a world of good.

A Man's Magic Meal

Plan ahead for the day when nothing short of an all-out rescue will save you. Most men have at least one meal they find easy to prepare. Ask the man in your life to share his specialty meal with you. Then, *always* have the ingredients on hand. This is your contribution to the magic-making.

When you need help—yell. Who knows? This special person may have been secretly hoping for an opportunity to dazzle you with his skills.

MAGIC MENU	ITEMS TO HAVE ON HAND
_____	_____
_____	_____
_____	_____
_____	_____
_____	_____

Pad to Fit

If you need a little more absorption from Baby's diaper now that he is larger, try adding an extra diaper, one you have folded into a size just right for covering the critical area. This will allow you to maintain the fit of a single diaper with the absorbent ability of two.

Window Safety

If you live in an old house with wide window sills, prepare now for the safety of your crawling, climbing baby. Adjustable gates can be used across these windows to protect Baby from the hazards of glass and screening. This is particularly important for second-story windows.

Boy or Girl?

If mistaken identity regarding your baby really bugs you, try this solution. Neatly embroider across the seat of your child's pants the simple words, "I'm a girl" or "I'm a boy."

PARENTS, FRIENDS, AND ADMIRERS

Beware of the Beast

An admirer's friendliest, most loyal pet may not take kindly to an invitation by Baby. Babies often emit strange sounds and make quick movements that pets may misunderstand, causing them to become aggressive. Beware and be extra careful.

Meals on Wheels

When you are cooking and taking something special to Baby's house, don't forget him. He will enjoy your goodies, too. How about chicken noodle soup? Baby loves noodles plain, or with a touch of butter. Or how about some of the stew vegetables—

mashed, of course. Or some applesauce made from the leftover apples you used for the apple pie.

Family Pictures

When you're exchanging pictures of the family, don't overlook Baby. He will enjoy pictures of his admirers as much as they like snapshots of him. Big ones are especially good.

Something from the Oven

Would you like to make goodies for your favorite baby? How about some freshly baked graham squares. Try our highly acclaimed recipe. Babies who have sampled them find them irresistible.

3½ cups graham flour (unbleached, unsifted)
½ tsp. baking powder
1 tsp. salt
1 tsp. cinnamon
¼ lb. butter
¼ cup brown sugar
¼ cup honey
1 tsp. vanilla
¾ cup water

1. Mix flour, baking powder, salt, and cinnamon.
2. Cream butter, sugar, and honey until light and fluffy. Then, add vanilla.
3. Alternating water and flour, add to butter mixture. Beat well after each addition.
4. Cover dough and allow to stand at room temperature for 30 minutes.
5. Divide dough in half. Place dough on a lightly greased cookie sheet; pat into a ½-in. thick rectangle. With floured rolling pin, roll dough almost to the edge of sheet. Using a pastry wheel or knife cut lines in the dough.
6. Bake at 325° F for 30 minutes or until brown.

Yield: 40 3-in. squares.

Poem

Here is another way to send a personal greeting. This verse, which might well become a keepsake, is easy to write. The style, called Haiku, refers to an unrhymed Japanese poem of three lines. Haiku often contains a seasonal motif.

Here is how you do it:

First line   5 syllables
Second line 7 syllables
Third line   5 syllables

Oh, darling baby
A joy to all of us now
Bloom in the sunshine.

YOURS:

_____

_____

_____

Jewelry

Ever wonder why grandmothers are such a hit with babies? It may be because they are such a visual treat, especially when it comes to accessories. Those touches of costume jewelry—brooches, buttons, and buckles—have great eye appeal. Baby is captivated by a sparkling pair of earrings or a tinkling bracelet.

Needlework

It's not too late for an admirer to embroider something special for Baby. An heirloom of this type is always appreciated. Handwork is a lifetime treasure, not only for Baby, but for Baby's babies, too.

Vegetable Special

Instead of a doll or a teddy bear or even another cuddly animal, how about something from the garden—a stuffed fabric vegetable? A plump pea or a tempting tomato can be purchased, or you can make one yourself.

Artist's Plate and Cup

Now that Baby is eating more and more "people food," a friend, especially a young one, might enjoy creating a mug or plate just for him. Your artist can draw, decorate, or design on a special surface using the crayons or markers that come as part of a kit. Some kits come prepared with a cup and saucer ready for design. Others provide paper and marking pens/pencils; upon completing the design, the artist sends the design to the company where it is reproduced onto the cup and saucer.

Invite this friend to create a mug for herself or himself so that she or he can share a snack or light meal with Baby. Check local craft stores for details.

Prints and Postcards

Make something special to send to friends who would appreciate early evidences of Baby's art. One of a kind, yours and Baby's alone, are the prints that come from thumbs. No two thumbprints have ever been found to be exactly alike.

Make your own ink pad; use a small hunk of sponge or an absorbent, folded piece of fabric that has been saturated with food coloring.

Press Baby's thumb down on the printing surface and then onto paper. Give the print a minute or so to dry.

The fun comes by adding lines, squiggles, and dots to your blob. Books on thumbprint drawings of all kinds are available—faces, animals, insects, and action designs.

Memo

Why is it that you inevitably spot things that would be "perfect" for Baby in a few months only when you are not looking or buying? As you discover them, make a note of these "finds" so that they are on file when you *are* ready to buy.

ITEM	STORE/LOCATION	COST
_____	_____	_____
_____	_____	_____
_____	_____	_____
_____	_____	_____

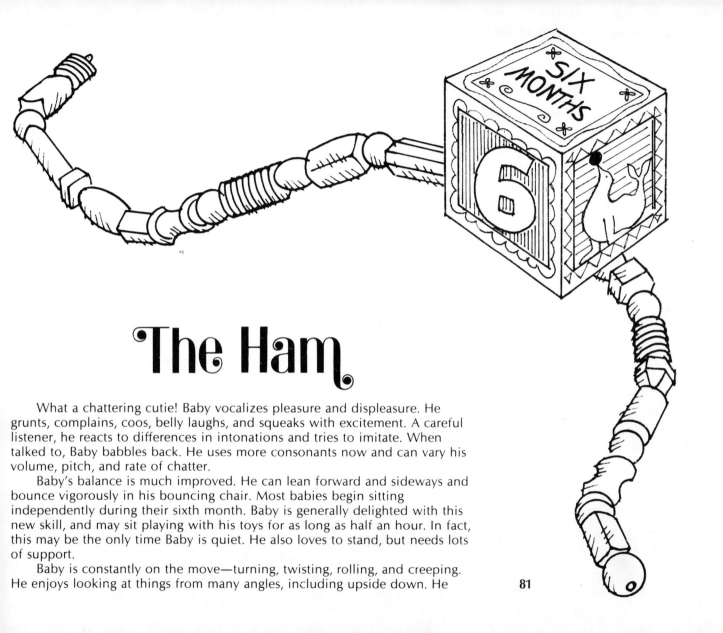

The Ham

What a chattering cutie! Baby vocalizes pleasure and displeasure. He grunts, complains, coos, belly laughs, and squeaks with excitement. A careful listener, he reacts to differences in intonations and tries to imitate. When talked to, Baby babbles back. He uses more consonants now and can vary his volume, pitch, and rate of chatter.

Baby's balance is much improved. He can lean forward and sideways and bounce vigorously in his bouncing chair. Most babies begin sitting independently during their sixth month. Baby is generally delighted with this new skill, and may sit playing with his toys for as long as half an hour. In fact, this may be the only time Baby is quiet. He also loves to stand, but needs lots of support.

Baby is constantly on the move—turning, twisting, rolling, and creeping. He enjoys looking at things from many angles, including upside down. He

81

loves playing peek-a-boo, especially if you create a version that involves movement.

Baby is most content when he is holding something and can transfer his treasure from hand to hand. His grasp has become quite sure; he can hold his own bottle. He can also reach to grasp with one hand now.

Mirrors top the list of baby entertainers. Baby now differentiates himself from the mirror image. He also loves music: listening and dancing to records, singing with others, and making music with toy instruments begin to be favorite activities. Baby has also noticed people writing. He can be entertained and fascinated just by watching you write.

Baby's favorite toys are the people close to him. He loves other babies but may be wary of adult strangers. He can now use his voice to get attention and will yell for help when frightened.

Routines are becoming more reliable. By now, Baby is well established on some solid foods. He enjoys trying to feed himself with finger foods and is starting to manipulate his cup. Best of all, this busy, sociable baby sleeps through the night.

ACTIVITIES, GAMES, AND SONGS

Edible Games

A few cheese squares, bits of crisp toast or banana, dry cereal shapes, or other tempting morsels can be placed in a clear plastic bottle or in a little gift box. Baby will enjoy playing with these containers, and in trying to open them he will be practicing his fine-motor skills. He will be delighted, too, to find this game has such a delicious ending.

Easy-Grasp Blocks

Babies love handles and flaps that make toys easier to grasp. Blocks with easy-grasp handles are simple to make. Start with a square of foam rubber. Cover each face of the block with a fabric circle. Simply glue the overlapping fabric around the blocks. This overlap fabric will allow for a rounded flap on each block edge.

Right-Side Up

Baby will enjoy showing everyone that he knows things have a right-side up. A great game to play is to place things at different angles and let Baby right them: shoes, cups, teddy bear—and don't leave out Baby and yourself as things to be righted!

Baby cannot always put himself in the position he would like and this can be frustrating. Now that he knows when things are right-side up, he will enjoy seeing the world from many different angles.

Who, Me?

Now that Baby responds to his name, be sure to call him often. He's delighted with this new skill, too.

Where's the Baby?

"Where's the Baby?" and other such search-and-find games are baby-pleasers. Get down on the floor, crawl around, and search for Baby. Call out, "Where is Baby? Where's the baby?" Ask others if they've seen Baby. Look under and around and near Baby. Finally, find him. "Here's Baby!" The more animated you are, the more fun! Soon Baby will learn to scramble away in delight as the game begins. He will laugh loudly and anticipate being found.

A Ball for Baby

Give Baby a tennis ball. This round, fuzzy little ball will be a favorite thing to carry. It is fun to drop several in boxes or cans. "Dead" tennis balls are perfectly acceptable to Baby. On the court or off, these balls are a hit.

Knee Game

A must is a ride on somebody's knee. Try this classic while singing or reciting:

Ride a cock horse
To Banbury Cross
To see a fine lady
Upon a white horse.
With rings on her fingers
And bells on her toes,
She shall have music
Wherever she goes.

Don't Pick Him Up Yet!

Because of his interest in finding out about things, Baby can play happily by himself for twenty to thirty minutes. Enjoy this phase while it lasts! When Baby gets restless, a change in position or a new toy will do.

Gotcha!

A perfect toy to chase is an aluminum-foil pie plate. This inexpensive and recycled item from your kitchen is fun to push, grasp, bang, throw, and chew. Baby will relentlessly stalk this toy as he improves his creeping. Add a face made of plastic-tape strips or turn it into a UFOB (unidentified flying object for Baby)—a disk from outer space.

Baby's Own

When you put safety latches on low kitchen cabinets and cupboards to keep your inquisitive infant out of harm's way, save some kitchen space just for him. (Remember, even with safety latches, tops for all potentially harmful items should be baby-proofed.) Let him know what is his by tying a bell or noisemaker to his special cabinet door. With this incentive, Baby will find added delight in opening and closing his own cabinet. Be sure to put some of Baby's favorite toys, or kitchen utensils you have chosen just for him, inside.

The Barnstorming Baby

For the infant who enjoys a different slant or perspective on his world, try a few gentle aerial feats. Rotate him upside down and roll him through space like a stunt plane. Listen for his squeals of delight. A few zooming sounds add to the fun—after all, you are the pilot, at least for now.

Another Old Favorite

Two Little Dicky-Birds

Two little dicky-birds
  (use index fingers to represent the birds)
Sitting on a wall,
One named Peter, the other named Paul
  (lift one finger for each bird).
Fly away, Peter; fly away, Paul
  (put each finger behind your back).
Come back, Peter; come back, Paul
  (bring each finger back).

Your Own Kind of Music

By now, you've done a lot of singing. You've developed some rather good numbers and Baby has crooned along. So now, before you forget the words, record your own music below.

_____

_____

_____

_____

_____

_____

Better yet, tape record a few of your favorites for your and Baby's enjoyment.

Cans

Add the shimmer of silver to Baby's toy collection by saving a series of cans. Once opened, emptied, washed, and dried, check the interiors for rough edges. Try three tuna cans in the 3-, 7-, and 13-oz. sizes. The cans in which tomato paste, puree, and sauce come are good, too.

You can cover the cans with colorful fabric, contact paper, or pictures under clear contact paper.

Or, make a graduated stacking-puzzle by attaching drawings to or painting three graduated cans. Use the smallest size for the head, the middle- and large-sized ones for the body. One parent made a snowman, another created a robot.

Talking Time

When you need a peaceful moment, place Baby in front of a mirror. He will chatter to his image endlessly, just as he talks to you.

Place the mirror low enough for Baby to pat his image, and make sure the mirror cannot tip over. Some parents put mirrors on baseboards, where Baby will see himself as he crawls. We like the commercial non-glass mirrors available in most toy stores.

Infant Obstacle Course

Gather together several towels, throw pillows, and stuffed toys. Lay them on the floor in variously sized piles. Now top with a blanket or a large sheet. Baby will enjoy this new, interesting terrain with things to creep around, over, and push off from—a challenging obstacle course for Baby.

Baby Mystery

If you have a non-glass double boiler, let Baby try to put it together. It's an intriguing mystery. It's a perfect early stacking toy for Baby. An old stove-top percolator can also present a challenge for Baby.

Tummy Tickler

A little tummy tickler is always a favorite baby game. These silly little rhymes are only a mechanism for helping infants learn the fun of anticipating something to come. Use this rhyme or invent your own.

Jelly in the bowl (shake Baby's tummy)
Jelly in the bowl (shake Baby's tummy)
Wiggle, waggle (sway him by his shoulders)
Wiggle, waggle (sway him by his shoulders)
Jelly in the bowl (tickle delighted Baby).

Photo Finish

Capture your busy and mature six-month-old at play. What a change six months can make!

Box Table

You can make a sturdy baby-sized work table from a cardboard box. Select a box that allows you to slip Baby in his infant seat under one side, forming a desk or tabletop. The box should be lying on its side with the top flap against the floor. The weight of the infant seat will hold the table steady. Now, to the

surface that will serve as the top of Baby's table, add a little edge or rim. This will keep Baby's work materials from sliding off.

ROUTINE TIMES

BATHING

Bath Toys

Keep an eye out for new bath toys. Seasonal gift catalogs are usually fine sources. Keep bathtime fun.

Boats

Inexpensive plastic boats may turn out to be no bargain. Many of these toys do not really float; they sink and allow water to be trapped inside, which can breed mildew.

Wooden boats, although more expensive, are more seaworthy and durable. They will last throughout Baby's preschool and primary years. Remember not to leave them sitting in water.

Making a few of these boats is a great project for a handy admirer.

Sponge boats have many nice features. They are easily made by simply cutting the boat parts from colorful sponges and then assembling the pieces with glue designed to withstand water. There need be no waste as the scraps can serve as decorations. These toys, which can be squeezed out after use, make bathing more fun if used as scrubbers.

No Slips

A bath mitt is handy for scrubbing a slippery baby. You can make your own by copying a kitchen hot mitt; use terry cloth or two washcloths.

Niagara Falls

While fun is to be encouraged during bathtime, splashing may not be as enjoyable for you as it is for Baby. Try wearing a thin, lightweight raincoat for complete coverage on days you'd rather stay dry.

Bath Bag

You can make a handy carryall in a few minutes from a face towel and plastic coat hanger. Flip the short side of the towel in so that a small triangle is formed on either side of the hanger hook. Stitch securely close to the hook.

To form the "bag," fold the towel in half bringing the lower edge up and over the horizontal hanger bar. Stitch close to the hanger and you have a great holder for bath toys.

FEEDING

Bottles and Cups

Baby is beginning to manipulate his own bottle. Sometimes he is even able to manage a cup. Encourage either or both of these skills. Although Baby still relies on the bottle for nourishment, practice with the cup is an important advance that should be supported. Let him practice drinking in the tub, where spills don't matter.

What Baby's Eating/When

A.M.   ITEMS

_____   _____

_____   _____

_____   _____

P.M.   ITEMS

_____   _____

_____   _____

_____   _____

Cleanup

There is no way to totally control the inevitable mess that occurs while feeding Baby; the only hope is to speed cleanup. Among the easiest possible ways are spreading out newspaper under the high chair and draping Baby in an oilcloth poncho.

Meals with Music

Baby loves music, now as never before. He will stop to listen to almost any type of music, reason enough for you to set the mood at mealtimes. Try presenting the classics if he's only heard the "Top 40," or country and western if he's listened only to jazz. It should contribute to more tolerable mealtimes.

Not Eating for You?

Without warning, Baby may suddenly decide to eat better for anyone but you. So *do* let fathers, friends, and siblings help. Sit back, relax, and enjoy.

Feeding Tips

Many parents and friends think that the only place to feed Baby is the high chair—not so. Just as you enjoy a change—spreading out a blanket for a picnic or sitting on low cushions for an Oriental meal—so does Baby. If you're finding it hard to contain an active Baby in his high chair, consider his jumping seat. The seat gives him an outlet for his energy and may allow you to get more of his meal into Baby.

Dual Feeding

Make mealtime a participatory experience for both you and Baby. Giving him something to do while you are feeding him may make this task somewhat easier. Food items he can handle on his own include banana disks and dried cereal pieces.

Convenience Food

If you like yogurt, you may discover that your infant does, too. A real convenience food, yogurt is easy to make or to purchase in economically sized containers. Finely chopped fruits or vegetables (fresh or cooked) add appeal and nutrition.

Yogurt can be breakfast, lunch, dinner, or a snack. Portable, too, yogurt can travel to day care or Grandma's house.

SLEEPING

Bad Habit

Many parents have found, much to their dismay, that what started as a good idea became something they wish they had never begun. We are referring to the practice of taking Baby back into your bed. Baby may, after the second or third time, actively look forward to this chance to be with you. He may awaken in the middle of the night and demand to join you. Don't give in. Check to see that he is safe, turn off the light, and leave. Being too responsive can encourage bedtime games. A change in Baby's routine can quickly become a habit.

Wee Baby Moon

This is a delightful song or poem to share with your child:

There's a wee baby moon
Just a-lyin' on his back
With his little tiny toes in the air.
And he's all by himself
In the deep blue sky
But the funny little moon doesn't care.

With Baby, any tune will do. He will enjoy and appreciate your efforts. It doesn't matter if your voice is flat or sharp—just be natural and try.

DRESSING AND CHANGING

Transitional Game

If Baby is engrossed in play or motor activity, you may find that he resists your efforts to diaper or change him. To make him more cooperative, try playing a game such as "Gotcha."

Fist Problems

One way to keep an impatient baby's hands busy while you proceed with the dressing process is to simply give him something to hold in each hand. This same idea can make dressing Baby in his bulky snowsuit easier, too. When you give Baby things to hold, make sure they are small so that you won't have a problem with sleeves. How about pieces of fabric, or celery leaves on which he can munch.

Finding and pulling a tightly clenched fist through a sleeve is far easier than trying to force the sleeve over an open hand. It also eliminates the possibility of bending tiny fingers the wrong way.

Work Clothes

Because Baby is entering a more active phase, why not replace his kimonos and creepers with sturdy overalls or coveralls. He'll enjoy this graduation to long pants and so will you. These new work clothes will afford Baby the protection and freedom he now requires. Believe it or not, they do make blue jeans, farmer's overalls, and workman's coveralls in Baby's size.

HELPFUL HINTS

Reminder

Baby will let you know when he wants company. He's very social now. Just watching you work is as absorbing and interesting as a new toy.

Recycling

Recycle some of Baby's earlier toys. Every time he reaches a new level of development, he regards familiar items with new insight. A block once used for carrying is now something to bang or drop. When Baby seems to tire of a toy, put it away for later. When you bring it out again, Baby will treat it as a new discovery.

A Planter with a Plus

Add a touch of green to Baby's room by hanging a green plant in a toy planter. Consider a fire truck with ivy or a doll buggy filled with fern. This is one way to use and admire Baby's special gifts until he is old enough to enjoy them.

Shining Brightly

If Baby received a traditional silver cup, mug, spoon, or rattle, now is the right time to catch his eye with the sheen of polished metal.

Place the item in a large aluminum container. Add 1 tablespoon of baking soda to each quart of water. Leave the silver piece immersed for 15 minutes. Rinse in hot water and dry. (Note: this method is not recommended for antiqued silverware.)

Larger Is Better

Everything that Baby finds goes directly to his mouth—everything and anything! Do check his toys to make sure there are no small parts that may be removed by this determined workman. Larger toys are best now—things to bang, shake, and throw.

Hide a Stain

If one of Baby's garments has a nonremovable stain, hide it with a colorful appliqué from the fabric store. The stitched-on appliqué will be a delightful eye-catcher, sure to please Baby and his admirers.

Jumping

A jumping seat or walker may be of real value this month. In these, Baby will be safe and yet not too confined at those times you just can't watch him so closely. Make sure the chair is well balanced. In later months, you may want to weight the chair for added stability.

Emergency Rations

Most babies travel in the back seat of the car where they are safer than they would be next to the driver. Sometimes the back seat is not acceptable to Baby and, on longer errands, he may begin to wail. If talking, singing, and the radio fail to do the trick, stop and pull out your trusty tin of crackers, which you keep in the glove compartment for just this purpose. It may help you both get home safe and sane.

Less Mess

Petroleum jelly in a plastic squeeze bottle makes it easy for you to handle this gooey substance less and ensure that you get a more precise amount on just the right spot.

Phone Calls

If Baby's not hungry, a sprinkle or two of baby powder or cornstarch on his high-chair tray will keep him happy and busy while you make a phone call. A dab of baby lotion can also be an interesting distraction.

Sparkling Bottles

Baby's food jars and bottles can sparkle with just a bit of extra effort. To keep them clean and clear, add a few pinches of borax to the dishwater and proceed as usual.

The First Tooth

Some babies get their first teeth, usually the lower central incisors, as early as four months. Boys seem to cut teeth somewhat earlier than girls.

_____

Baby's name

_____

Date

_____

First tooth (location)

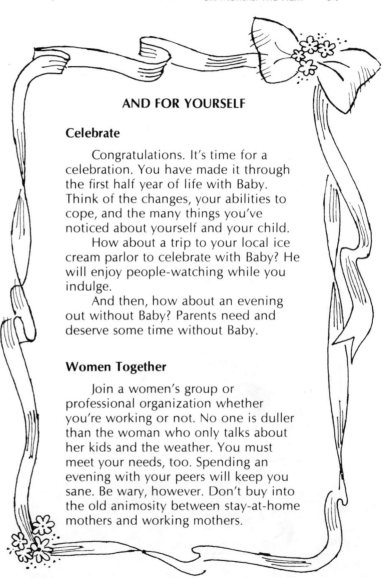

AND FOR YOURSELF

Celebrate

Congratulations. It's time for a celebration. You have made it through the first half year of life with Baby. Think of the changes, your abilities to cope, and the many things you've noticed about yourself and your child.

How about a trip to your local ice cream parlor to celebrate with Baby? He will enjoy people-watching while you indulge.

And then, how about an evening out without Baby? Parents need and deserve some time without Baby.

Women Together

Join a women's group or professional organization whether you're working or not. No one is duller than the woman who only talks about her kids and the weather. You must meet your needs, too. Spending an evening with your peers will keep you sane. Be wary, however. Don't buy into the old animosity between stay-at-home mothers and working mothers.

Teething

Research does not substantiate the claim that teething causes diarrhea. Like the common cold, diarrhea is passed on by germs. If Baby develops persistent diarrhea, consult your doctor. Nor does research substantiate the claim that teething causes a significant temperature of 101° F or so.

Pretzel Teethers

None of the fine Philadelphia-born-and-bred babies we know would be caught without their Pennsylvania Dutch pretzels. These pencil-thick, hard snacks are preferred over crackers and other teething biscuits. Our young friends gnaw, nibble, and bang these pretzels, which fortunately rarely crumble into a mushy mess. Saltless pretzels are best; just brush the salt off before giving to Baby.

A Spoon for the Teether

Dusting a wooden spoon, one of Baby's favorite toys, with a little powdered sugar might bring a smile to a teething sufferer.

Drooling

Babies drool when teething; some drool more than others. Here are some suggestions for coping with a drooler. The obvious ones are:

—small bibs
—"total body" aprons

—_____
(Yours)

Less obvious ones include:

—a cowboy's bandana
—a handkerchief strategically tucked inside the front of Baby's shirt
—a little spray-on fabric guard secretly and subtly applied to the front of Baby's best duds

Drooling will not end until Baby's teeth arrive.

Freezer Tip

Teething is no fun. Remember your last toothache? Anything that will cheer Baby up or make him more comfortable is well worth your time and effort. Experiment to see what seems to help. One suggestion is a hard rubber toy, one that can be made more effective as a teething device by being placed in the freezer for an hour before use. Special toys made for freezing can also be bought.

New Life

Tired of the pale pink, yellow, orange, and brown stains on Baby's little, almost white, T-shirts? A quick remedy and one that will bring Baby into the fashion spotlight is to dye them in fabulous fall shades. Easier to use than the dyes you remember, today's dyes are safe, inexpensive, and simple to use. For the craft-fair look, remember tie-dying. Bunch fabric and wrap with rubber bands or tie at intervals with string. For vibrant color, used prepared liquid dye at double strength.

Quick Dispenser

Sometimes it is easy to overlook the obvious. A mother recently shared an idea that seemed so simple we were amazed we had never thought of it. She had installed a toilet-paper dispenser near the changing table. What could be a better choice for cleaning Baby's tender bottom than soft toilet tissue? A paper-towel dispenser would also be a good idea. Not only is this a very convenient and sanitary system, but it is far less costly than commercially packaged baby wipes.

PARENTS, FRIENDS, AND ADMIRERS

Color

The latest polls reveal that red is still Baby's favorite color. Think bright when you select clothes for your child or someone else's. How about a pair of glorious red socks for tiny feet? Or maybe a pair of warm mittens or a cozy hat?

Old Pros

Since you have been a successful parent/friend/caregiver for six months, why not share some of your insights and triumphs with folks who have just begun. One way might be a chain letter describing helpful hints and time-savers. Here is how to begin.

Write out your tip and a list of three friends and their addresses with your name at the top of the list. Send these to six other friends instructing them to send their helpful hint to the top name on the enclosed list of names. They should then remove the name of the person to whom they send the tip and place their own name on the bottom of the list.

Centers and Sitters

Parents who take Baby to a day-care center or baby-sitter should not view this as only a paid, professional service. You pay for the care of your child, but all the love he receives there comes free. Thoughtful parents quickly recognize this and realize that any addition they make to this environment benefits Baby.

Since most of Baby's waking hours are spent at the center, why keep all of Baby's toys at home? Sending in toys you're willing to share with all the babies and which you do not expect returned is only logical. Suggestions of things to send include mobiles, crib gyms, learning toys, safety mirrors, and a batch of graham crackers. Even a little chocolate pudding for a finger-painting experience or a jar of hand cream for Baby's caring friends says you understand and appreciate the loving kindness these people are giving your baby and your family. Do return it in kind.

Toys

Find yourself with a baby who is bored without his favorite toys? Or, perhaps a baby who is unexpectedly visiting needs a little something with which to play. Present Baby with a piece of colored tissue paper, aluminum foil, or cellophane and watch the fun. Make sure he doesn't eat these items!

Joyride

Baby is very attracted to social play with his admirers. Make a sliding board out of your legs and help Baby get up and down. Here's a little rhyme to accompany Baby.

Slide, Baby, slide
Now it's time to ride
Up here on my knees
Anytime you please.
Come now let's have fun
We have just begun.

Get Down, Too

Because of their willingness to get down on the floor and romp with Baby, men seem to be favorite playmates. Baby enjoys gentle rough-and-tumble.

T-shirt Togetherness

The matched look for your favorite family could be matching T-shirts with or without logos. These could be real pieces of nostalgia, particularly if captured in an admirable historic photo.

Thoughtfulness

One sister-in-law told us that her in-laws kept her in contact with the world while she was recuperating and adjusting to life with her baby. About every other week, her mother-in-law would send a letter and a little envelope of clippings from current magazines, newspapers, and books. This interesting assortment was greatly appreciated by the new mother, who was too busy to read a whole book or magazine, much less hunt down a tasty new recipe.

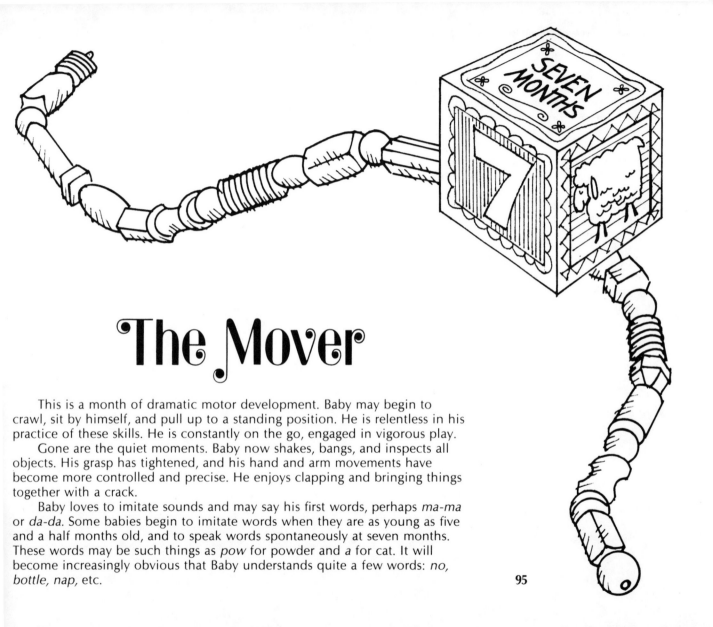

The Mover

This is a month of dramatic motor development. Baby may begin to crawl, sit by himself, and pull up to a standing position. He is relentless in his practice of these skills. He is constantly on the go, engaged in vigorous play.

Gone are the quiet moments. Baby now shakes, bangs, and inspects all objects. His grasp has tightened, and his hand and arm movements have become more controlled and precise. He enjoys clapping and bringing things together with a crack.

Baby loves to imitate sounds and may say his first words, perhaps *ma-ma* or *da-da*. Some babies begin to imitate words when they are as young as five and a half months old, and to speak words spontaneously at seven months. These words may be such things as *pow* for powder and *a* for cat. It will become increasingly obvious that Baby understands quite a few words: *no, bottle, nap,* etc.

95

By this month, Baby has learned to discriminate between different familiar faces. Categories of recognition are also developing. Baby can often tell the difference between men and women, or boys and girls, but not yet between two women or two men unless, of course, they are close friends or family.

The seventh month may also bring another heralded event—Baby's first tooth. The lower incisors generally come in first. At this stage, infrequent fussiness might be due to teething.

Baby is now beginning to make associations and to anticipate his routines. When his bib is put on, he knows that food will come. He demands some independence during mealtimes and may refuse to relinquish his spoon and cup. Finger foods are a welcome compromise for both Baby and adult.

Baby will display some new emotions at this age. Your social seven-month-old infant will want to be a part of the grown-up world. He can tease and is beginning to have a sense of humor. He remembers bits of games and invites friends to play with him. But, confronted by strangers, your outgoing, vocal infant may show "stranger anxiety," a very normal reaction.

ACTIVITIES, GAMES, AND SONGS

Seeing Me

Mirrors continue to be among Baby's favorite toys. He is recognizing himself. Make sure there is an accessible mirror for an admiring Baby. If Baby is sitting up, place a mirror where he can see himself eat and bathe. This will fascinate him.

Baby Talk

Playing back a recording of Baby's chatter can be lots of fun for everyone. Years from now your child will love hearing it himself.

Eyes, Nose, and Mouth Game

One of Baby's best games is to point to his eyes, nose, and mouth (with your help). Played in front of a mirror this game is especially fun. Soon Baby will learn to recognize the words and associate them with the correct features.

A Ball for Baby

Try a small colorful beach ball. Baby will enjoy holding it, having it rolled to him, or crawling after it.

Mouth Harp

Mickey was able to play on a harmonica at seven months. He enjoyed using both draw and blow notes up and down the scale. His parents said they merely demonstrated how to play and were delighted when Mickey imitated them. Don't underestimate Baby's interests. Mickey still delights his day-care center with his daily playing.

First House

A large cardboard box can be converted into a great A-frame playhouse. Simply remove two opposing sides of the box and the top. Leave the bottom attached. Securely tape the remaining sides together so that you now have a triangular structure. Cut large holes out of the sides for windows. You can paint the house with latex enamel. Baby will enjoy crawling through, peeking out of, and sitting in his house.

Bubbles

Take out your jar of bubbles again. It can provide lots of fun for Baby when you need a different activity and have a few moments to spare. Bubbles never seem to lose their appeal.

Bare-footing

Assemble a variety of textures in a path; use a rug sample, grass mat, bath mat, pillow, etc. With your help, Baby will enjoy toddling and crawling across these various surfaces.

Peek-a-Boo

Baby is now ready to play this game in many ways. For variety, you can place your hands over his eyes, hide from Baby, put something in front of Baby's face (diaper, magazine), or stand behind the door and peek out. These easy variations will delight Baby.

High-Chair Fishing

Objects and toys on elastic strips are one way to save your back, since everything Baby touches ends up on the floor! The elastic lets Baby play a fishing game—throw away the toy, then reel it in.

Kitchen Collection

Cooking equipment makes an intriguing collection of toys. Pots, pans, and lids are popular, as are wooden bowls and spoons, measuring cups, whisks, plastic cups and saucers, plastic bottles, and ice cube trays.

Place Baby on the kitchen floor, a safe distance from your working area, surrounded by these toys. You'll find that you are able to get your work done and that Baby will be working right along with you.

Wrappings

A box of fancy cards, bits of wrapping paper, pretty fabric, wallpaper scraps, and ribbon can captivate Baby's interest in detail.

Finger Painting

Place Baby in his high chair. Put about one tablespoonful of chocolate pudding on his tray and stand back! Baby will enjoy tasting, patting, smearing, and creating an artistic design on his tray. You can save his earliest efforts by quickly blotting up the design with a piece of paper.

Roll Toy

A metallic, egg-shaped container for panty hose can make a great roll toy. Put some bells, sand, beans, or rice inside and seal carefully with a strong glue. Tape securely shut for good measure. Baby will enjoy chasing this shiny bauble.

Puzzle

Even a seven-month-old can benefit from puzzle play. Simply screw small wooden cabinet knobs

(½ in.) purchased at your hardware store into several blocks. Arrange these blocks so they fit snugly into a cardboard box. Baby will enjoy taking them out of the box and putting them back in.

Easy Blocks

You can make a set of durable and wipeable blocks from a variety of milk cartons. Using two milk cartons, fit the bottom ends together and cut off the tops. Cover with colorful contact paper; Baby especially likes prints. If you add some beans or bells, Baby will enjoy rattling and banging these blocks together.

Kitchen Drum

A saucepan and two fat carrots make a great drum set. This is a good game to promote when you must be in the kitchen. Invite a sibling to join Baby.

Step Blocks

Baby is now interested in climbing stairs, much to the horror of all concerned. After all, there are motor skills to be learned from the challenge of negotiating stairs. If you do not have a set of preschool stairs on which Baby can safely practice, make a set out of cardboard boxes stacked and secured in formation. Fill several boxes (approximately 6 in. x 12 in. x 18 in.) with newspapers to weight them. Seal the boxes and cover with colorful contact paper. Baby can now safely practice.

Dumping

Baby loves to dump things. A wide-mouthed, plastic, five-gallon jar filled with a variety of things to dump and pull out—clothespins, cups, blocks—soon becomes a favorite toy. When Baby is finished, the loose items can be neatly stored in the jar.

Puppy Toys

Soft rubber toys designed for puppies are excellent for babies, too. They squeak easily. Their softness makes them easy to hold. Many puppy toys have unusual textures and vibrant colors.

Does this idea sound familiar? We did suggest buying these cute critters earlier. Remember, Baby will enjoy using them in different ways now. He will bang them, throw them, and stuff them into other toys or clothing.

Walking with You

Hold both Baby's hands and he will enjoy strutting as you let him practice walking. Baby never tires of this game.

Pat-a-Cake

Now that Baby can clap his hands, "Pat-a-Cake" is a favorite.

Pat-a-cake, pat-a-cake,
Baker's man;
Bake me a cake
As fast as you can.
Pat it and prick it
And mark it with B,
And put it in the oven
For Baby and me.

Do the motions with Baby as you chant the verse.

View from the Floor

Baby likes to look at pictures, too. Drawings or photographs, especially those of other babies, puppies, and cats, will enrich his visual environment.

Hang the pictures at Baby's eye level. Clear contact paper protects special favorites. Completely seal the pictures for best results.

Oldies but Goodies

Finger stories have stood the test of time. All babies love them. Do you remember this one?

Knock at the door (forehead),
Peep in (peep through circled thumbs and
   forefingers),
Turn the latch (twist nose),
Walk in (put a finger into Baby's mouth).

Eency Weency Spider

An eency weency spider
Climbed up the water spout
   (one hand climbs up arm to shoulder).
Down came the rain
   (raise hands high in air and drop them down
   quickly)
And washed the spider out
   (hand slides down arm).
Out came the sun
   (arms form circle over head)
And dried up all the rain.
The eency, weency spider
   (hand goes back up arm to shoulder)
Climbed up the spout again.

At first, you will be doing the motions on Baby. He will be delighted and anticipate the movements. As he grows to know them, he will vocalize and eventually try to gesture.

Books

Don't forget to look at picture books with Baby. A good time for this activity is before nap- and bedtime. Looking at books in this way can set the tone for early learning. A desire to read starts with a love of books.

Sorting

A cupcake or muffin tin can be great for sorting pretzel nuggets or wooden blocks. Sometimes a finicky eater will be intrigued by morsels placed in these tins to retrieve and nibble. Try a few cheese squares, banana disks, or small teething biscuits.

Talking

Baby loves to chuckle and coo. He really thinks he can talk. It's not too early to let him try his conversational skills with you. Talk to him and he will answer. Often he will try to initiate the conversation, so be sure to answer.

Poker

It's time to bring out the wooden sorter boxes with holes through which to put blocks. Baby is learning to poke his little fingers into small places and loves it. Although Baby may not yet be able to put the blocks into the right holes, he will enjoy poking his fingers through the holes.

ROUTINE TIMES

Cause and Effect

Baby hears the water running and knows it's time for a bath. He perks up at the sound of familiar footsteps, he grows still at the mention of a nap, and calls when he needs assistance. All these examples reflect Baby's growing ability to recognize and anticipate the workings of his surroundings. Baby is taking a more active part in getting what he needs.

BATHING

Squeeze Bottles

Additions to the tub that will appeal to Baby are squeeze bottles. Thoroughly clean clear plastic detergent or colored food bottles such as those containing margarine, mustard, or syrup. Then, let Baby play with them in the tub.

Bathtime is the perfect time to experiment with dipping, squeezing, and squirting. Best of all, these free toys float.

Fingernails

As you've surely noticed, Baby's tiny fingernails, although almost transparent, can scratch delicate skin. Put a little powder or cornstarch under each nail and you will be able to see what you are cutting. As suggested earlier, this task is best done while Baby is sleeping.

Bathtime

No longer content to just sit in his bath, Baby needs the closest and most constant type of supervision. Protect him from a quick pull-up or an attempt to get out of the tub.

SLEEPING

Crib Comfort

A very crafty mom we know developed crib interest for her child in a most unusual way. She selected two sheets, one solid and one print. She then followed the design on the printed sheet and machine-quilted large forms. The result was a reversible sheet or comforter to amuse a restless seven-month-old who enjoyed tracing the puffy forms with his fingers while drifting off to sleep.

Bedcheck

Rachel's mom reminded us to check again when a seven-month-old is cranky at bedtime. Even though you've just changed him, Baby could be wet again. Urine, which becomes more acidic around this time, stings or burns, keeping Baby from settling down to sleep.

Shorter Naps

Baby's morning nap may be shorter now. Some babies will, over the next few months, be giving up their morning nap entirely. However, the need for sleep varies among children. Fill in the chart. This information can make naptime an easier process for you both regardless of the number of rest periods required by Baby.

Baby rests well when _____

_____

_____

What helps (toys, blankets, music, reading a story)?

_____

_____

_____

Baby prefers his body in _____

_____ position.

FEEDING

The Cup

Now is the time to start using a cup. A two-handled, weighted model is a good choice because there is more for Baby to hold. While his initial attempts may be disastrous, practice is important. If Baby is teething, a cup may be preferred because it places less pressure on tender gums. At the beginning, do use the special spill-proof lid; it will make this new experience easier.

First successful use of Baby's cup
(date and comments).

_____

_____

_____

Mealtimes

Feeding can be hectic now that Baby is fond of
spoons. One useful trick may be to have two spoons.
You hold yours while Baby holds his. Through a
process of frequent spoon exchanges you'll find that
you can get through the meal with minimal stress.

Endurance is the only real answer. It won't be
long before Baby can feed himself. Don't discourage
his efforts at self-help. Relax and try to appreciate
Baby's antics for what they are—steps toward
independence.

Bottle Straws

Bottle straws are very handy small plastic straws
that fit into the standard bottle nipples. They can be
easily used by a sitting baby and eliminate the need
for the bottle to be inverted at a special angle. Many
parents swear by them.

Finger Foods

This month marks the beginning of the great
escape for Baby's feeders. Baby will work hard and
enjoy the challenge of feeding himself. Beginning

goodies include toast, cheese bits, cooked potatoes,
green beans, carrots, zucchini, and asparagus, cut
into small pieces.

Food Preferences

LIKES | DISLIKES

_____ | _____

_____ | _____

_____ | _____

_____ | _____

_____ | _____

More Firsts

First food eaten successfully with fingers:

_____

_____

_____

_____

Traffic Patterns

With your social baby wanting to share his
mealtime with you, keep in mind the traffic pattern
in your kitchen or dining area. Plan ahead when

positioning Baby's chair. He will drop (or throw) occasional bits of food that will be tracked about the home unless you give him his special spot. A layer of newspaper, an oilcloth, or an old tablecloth under his chair can make cleanup easier. Baby may perform less when he doesn't have an audience of laughing family members.

Meat Matters

Baby is growing rapidly and needs his protein. Remember his meat. If necessary, mix it with his favorite vegetables or other preferred foods, but make sure he gets some meat daily. Cheese and fish are also good protein sources.

Babies don't have the same concerns as we do about what foods go together. Applesauce and spinach may be a special favorite.

DRESSING AND CHANGING

Getting a wiggly baby into clean clothes is often a tussle. Show him how he can participate in this ritual by grasping and pulling down his shirt or picking up his shoes or socks. You can chant this little rhyme while helping him:

Hurry Up

It's time for a change
And so much more.
When I'm dressed
I'll head for the floor.
So pull on my shirt
And cover my knees.
I'm ready to play,
So quick, if you please,
Slip on my socks
And forget the shoes,
Hurry up now
I've no time to lose.

Better Fit

If you are using disposable diapers and having leaks, remember that these diapers can be altered for a better fit. Pull out the accordion fold all the way. Then refold the diaper to the needed proportions before taping. Don't use a bigger-size diaper than you absolutely need. Although diapers with fitted legs are now available commercially, they are quite expensive.

Double Diaper

Yes, you can double diaper with disposable diapers. A mother who takes her baby home on the subway explained this little trick.

Put two diapers together, soft sides touching each other. Now cut away the plastic in the seat area of the top diaper. Add a diaper liner if Baby can't tolerate the remaining plastic against his skin. This arrangement allows the second diaper to draw most of the moisture during those long trips.

HELPFUL HINTS

Reminder

Take care . . . experts tell us that your tension can be transmitted to an infant. None of us enjoy all aspects of child care. That's why it's important that you take breaks and be good to yourself.

Newsletter

Practical-Parenting, a newsletter, is published six times a year. Subscriptions cost five dollars. Order yours from:

Meadowbrook Press
16648 Meadowbrook Lane
Wayzata, Minnesota 55391

Call Out

Vocal contact is comforting for Baby. If you leave the room, call often to Baby and let him know what you're doing and that you will return. Out of sight need not mean left alone.

Fancy Framing

Every baby receives special articles of clothing. Many are lovingly made or chosen, some are heirlooms, others are exotic or of foreign design. Once outgrown, or before their debut, show them off! Place these treasures inside a clear plastic box-type frame and hang on the wall for decoration in Baby's room.

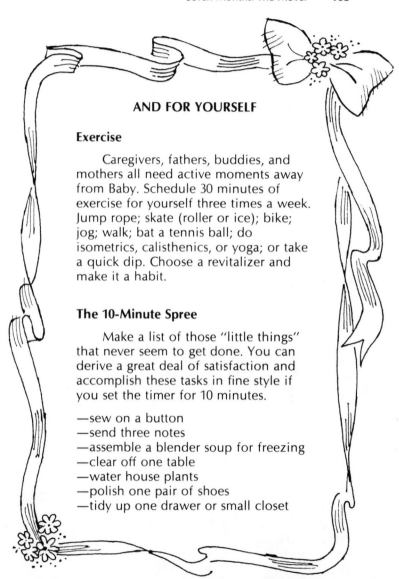

AND FOR YOURSELF

Exercise

Caregivers, fathers, buddies, and mothers all need active moments away from Baby. Schedule 30 minutes of exercise for yourself three times a week. Jump rope; skate (roller or ice); bike; jog; walk; bat a tennis ball; do isometrics, calisthenics, or yoga; or take a quick dip. Choose a revitalizer and make it a habit.

The 10-Minute Spree

Make a list of those "little things" that never seem to get done. You can derive a great deal of satisfaction and accomplish these tasks in fine style if you set the timer for 10 minutes.

—sew on a button
—send three notes
—assemble a blender soup for freezing
—clear off one table
—water house plants
—polish one pair of shoes
—tidy up one drawer or small closet

Pull-up

Baby may now begin to pull himself to a standing position. This is a signal for caregivers to rethink furniture arrangements. Furniture should be put away if Baby is strong enough to pull the pieces over on himself.

Taping Cords

Protect your exploring child and your furniture. Secure lamp cords with transparent tape close to furniture base.

Fussin' and Fallin'

Tumbles and bumps are part of exploring, learning, and playing. To minimize the tears, provide quick comfort. Sometimes Baby's reaction depends on yours. If you simply smile, Baby may shrug off his "injury" and start to laugh. If not, a pat, a hug, a kind word, and Baby will be back in action again.

Crafty Kid

Make a note of the first time your baby intentionally teased you.

_____

_____

_____

Who else has noticed? When did it happen?

_____

_____

_____

Hip Sling

Bokki's mom showed us a quick, colorful way to move around when a stroller is too cumbersome and hands are full. She used a piece of African fabric, draped it across her body, and tied it on her shoulder, making a sling in which her child could sit. Bokki could now sit comfortably, with one leg on each side of his mother's hip; he could ride safely, enjoying the nearness of his mom.

Stranger Anxiety

Babies need time to get acquainted with new people. You play an important part in this process. Don't be alarmed if your once happy baby becomes shy when approached by strangers. This normal reaction is quite common at seven months.

You can help Baby by sitting him on your lap while talking, giving Baby an opportunity to look the new person over before introducing him or her.

Pillow Play

Remember those cute T-shirts and other items that Baby outgrew (see Chapter 3)? Get them out, stitch all openings but one together, stuff with polyester filling, and close up the last opening for durable, colorful pillows. These toy-togs will serve as buffers in the playpen or crib; they are ideal for a baby who likes to toss or throw things.

Margin of Error

Everything takes longer now. Allowing enough time is essential if you are to keep your sense of humor.

On those days when being on time is crucial, tack an additional 30 minutes onto your preparation time and see what a difference it makes.

Egg Poacher

Use this handy kitchen appliance to keep the meal of the leisurely-eating seven-month-old warmed to the proper level. Salton and Oster both make easy-clean models.

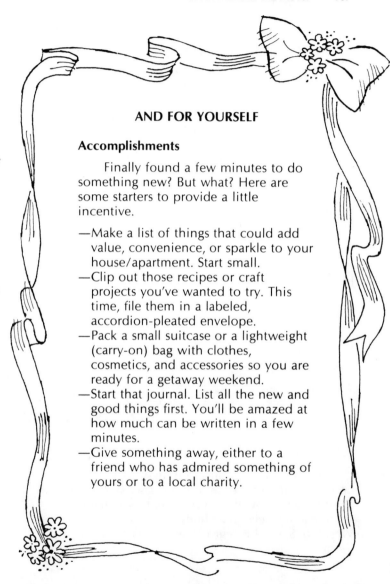

AND FOR YOURSELF

Accomplishments

Finally found a few minutes to do something new? But what? Here are some starters to provide a little incentive.

—Make a list of things that could add value, convenience, or sparkle to your house/apartment. Start small.
—Clip out those recipes or craft projects you've wanted to try. This time, file them in a labeled, accordion-pleated envelope.
—Pack a small suitcase or a lightweight (carry-on) bag with clothes, cosmetics, and accessories so you are ready for a getaway weekend.
—Start that journal. List all the new and good things first. You'll be amazed at how much can be written in a few minutes.
—Give something away, either to a friend who has admired something of yours or to a local charity.

Food-Carton Baby-Food Caddy

A handy way to store all those baby-food jars and keep them from getting lost in the refrigerator is the baby-food caddy. This organizer also limits the number of trips to the refrigerator when preparing meals. Look for small six-pack cartons (the type that hold single servings of mixers or wine). Cover the carton with bright contact paper or paint with latex enamel paint and you have your caddy.

Cleaner Toys

Stuffed toys look cleaner and brighter after an application of cornstarch. Rub the cornstarch into the soiled toy and set aside briefly. Remove the powder with a stiff brush.

Think Safety!

Very little will escape your baby's exploring hands. Careful babyproofing is a must at this stage. Strings and electric cords become irresistible; beware of everything in Baby's reach. It's not too early to start using safety plugs in all electric sockets.

Teething Tips

Here are some soothing suggestions for a baby with tender gums: a breadstick, a bagel necklace, a frozen carrot, a wooden clothespin (old-fashioned style), or a puppy's hard rubber ring.

Happy Hands

Prepare now for the inevitable accidents that will occur as Baby becomes more mobile. Nothing soothes a cranky teether or a baby bumped on the mouth like the Happy Hand. Fill a surgical glove with water, tie a knot at the end, and freeze. Children who may not want you to hold an ice cube over a sore will be more than willing to suck a finger or thumb of the Happy Hand. The thumb and fingers are the right size for a baby's mouth so the ice goes where it will do the most good.

PARENTS, FRIENDS, AND ADMIRERS

Baby Gallery

Did you save pictures from months 1, 3, and 5, or, better still, from each month? If so, select your favorites and blow them up for all to see. Baby will soon begin to recognize himself. Include a portrait of VIPs, too. Special caregivers deserve space in Baby's room.

Invitations

Grandparents can provide the young family with affordable ways to get away from home. A weekend invitation to visit grandparents who live out of town or an invitation to come for Sunday dinner are to be looked forward to; such events eliminate a great deal of hassle and stress. They also provide a large, very reassuring dose of admiration, appreciation, and loving support for the still less than self-confident new family.

Thrifty Tip

Check local papers or bulletin boards for best buys in toys and infant equipment. Kiddie gyms, jumper chairs, and pushtoys are worth looking and waiting for. Yard sales can be especially rewarding.

Quick Change

How long has it been since you changed Baby's surroundings? At seven months Baby is active, but also easily bored. Keep things lively, for both your sakes! Move the crib, bring in a plant or bouquet of flowers and place just out of Baby's reach. Tack up a big bright poster or two. Babies respond to primary colors. Don't forget the ceiling.

Quality Trip

A piggy-back ride on a taller person's shoulders is a good trip that *never* grows old. The view from the top is exciting.

I Love Daddy

According to some researchers, Baby prefers playing with Daddy at seven months. Apparently games with fathers tend to be more physical and, in this mobile month, Baby responds enthusiastically to such play.

For the Admirer, the Knee Ride

Here is a little game to play with Baby once you have become acquainted. Cross your knees and sit Baby on one side. Hold on to both his hands, bounce him to the rhyme, and on "Whoops" swing him by uncrossing your knees.

Leg over leg
A dog went to Dover.
He came to a wall—
Whoops—he jumped over.

Face Book

A special friend (sibling or child) might make a "Face Book" for Baby. Any face, animal or human, is suitable. To ensure durability, glue choices onto cardboard and then cover with clear contact paper; remember this book will be tasted, poked, and handled at lot.

Baby Loves Babies

Better than Mommy, another child, or special friend, is another baby. Just watch how infants intently observe and imitate each other's actions. They learn from each other. Now may be a good time to consider joining (or forming) a playgroup.

Playgroup

Join with three or four other parents to form a playgroup. Children within four months of each other will enjoy being together regularly for an hour or so two times a week. Because they are, after all, just babies, keep plans flexible and simple. Snacks or preparations should be completed before the group gathers. Limit the play area, closing off all other parts of the house. These occasions provide adults an opportunity to exchange stories, information, and tips on child care. Even at this tender age, the friendships formed often last for years.

To Grandma

Maybe it's not your luscious chocolate chip recipe, but it will receive rave reviews from all your favorite babies.

Grandma's Teething Biscuits

1 egg yolk, beaten
3 tbsp. honey
1 tsp. vanilla
1 cup flour
1 tbsp. quick-cooking oats
1 tbsp. powdered milk

1. Blend egg yolk, honey, and vanilla; then add dry ingredients. Dough will be stiff.
2. Roll out dough thinly and cut into finger length "T" or barbell shapes.
3. Bake at 350° F on an ungreased cookie sheet for 15 minutes.
4. Cool and store in an airtight container.

Makes about 2 dozen, depending on the shape used.

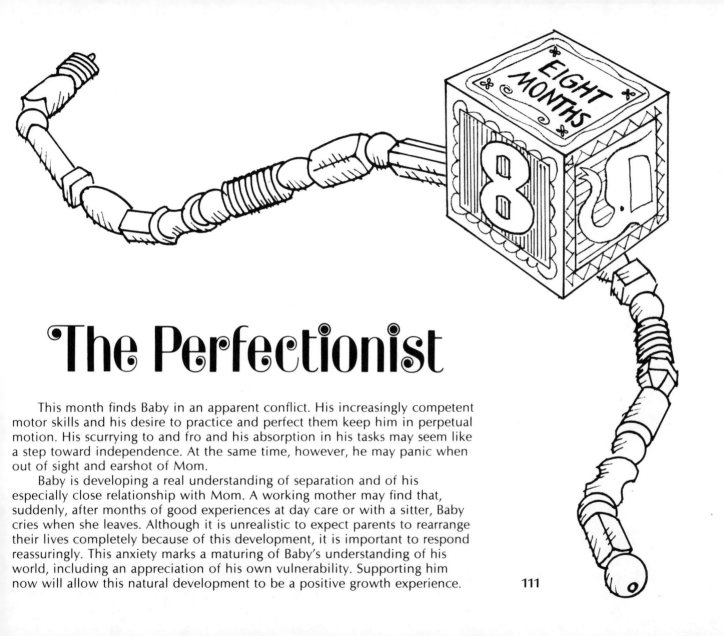

The Perfectionist

This month finds Baby in an apparent conflict. His increasingly competent motor skills and his desire to practice and perfect them keep him in perpetual motion. His scurrying to and fro and his absorption in his tasks may seem like a step toward independence. At the same time, however, he may panic when out of sight and earshot of Mom.

Baby is developing a real understanding of separation and of his especially close relationship with Mom. A working mother may find that, suddenly, after months of good experiences at day care or with a sitter, Baby cries when she leaves. Although it is unrealistic to expect parents to rearrange their lives completely because of this development, it is important to respond reassuringly. This anxiety marks a maturing of Baby's understanding of his world, including an appreciation of his own vulnerability. Supporting him now will allow this natural development to be a positive growth experience.

111

Baby will probably practice pulling up and standing this month. Unfortunately, he can't always get back down once he's on his feet. His attempts may include many falls, so protect him by padding areas where he is allowed to practice.

His drive to be mobile may actually wake Baby up at night. You may find him practicing pulling up in his crib. This will be particularly frustrating until he can get down and stops crying for help. You can try to teach Baby how to let himself down, but he will probably learn how all by himself. Once you are sure he can do it, be firm about these nighttime workouts. If you do not encourage him to stay awake, they will gradually cease.

Baby is now developing a true pincer grasp. Being able to handle objects with the thumb and forefinger is one characteristic that distinguishes humans from other animals. Baby will use this new skill in order to learn about his environment. Objects that are unsafe or that you want to protect must be put away for now.

Baby has been listening to you speak since birth. Words that have a special significance for him may crystallize in meaning for him this month so that he will understand them every time they are spoken. He may also develop "words" that have true meaning behind them, even if they don't seem to resemble words you know. Some babies do speak their first real words this month.

ACTIVITIES, GAMES, AND SONGS

Chase Game

One of Baby's greatest pleasures will be you imitating his style. So, down on all fours; Baby will take the lead and look to see if you are following. He'll squeal with delight as you chase and follow him about the room. "Here I come, I'm going to catch you!" Don't fail to hug and hold him close after he's been caught.

In and Through

Curious babies love challenging crawling experiences. Make a quick tunnel out of cardboard boxes. Another sure winner is to open a few suitcases and place them in different spots in one room. Put a few enticing items in each suitcase. Baby will crawl from one to another, sitting for a while in each.

Simon Says

Now that Baby uses gestures, he will enjoy games of imitation. He can do as you do but will like you doing as he does best. Simply observe until you see a gesture to repeat (table-patting, hand-waving, etc.). Now repeat this gesture exactly. It won't take long for Baby to catch on. His sudden beaming smile will convey his delight.

Pat the Pillow

A quick game for Baby can be fashioned from an old pillow. Sew four or five velcro tabs onto the pillow. Sew the other side of the tabs onto cloth shapes cut from a variety of colorful textured scraps. Baby will enjoy pulling off these scraps and patting them onto the pillow again. In time, he will be able to play this game alone.

Hide-and-Seek

"Hide-and-Seek" around an overstuffed chair or around the door can be great fun, especially if you're on your knees and crawling along with Baby. When you play this game, include others—teddy bears, dolls, and siblings.

A Ball for Baby

Baby will enjoy chasing a 4-in. rubber ball as he crawls around the floor.

Plates of Food

Do you have extra paper plates from a picnic? Cut out a few colorful pictures of food from magazines and glue them to the center of each plate. Now cover the pictures with a square of clear contact paper. Baby will enjoy sorting, stacking, touching, and mouthing these new toys.

It's Following Me!

For your crawler who likes to take something along on his excursions, toys with short strings that jangle as he crawls are special fun. These pull toys are easy to make from an assortment of whatever is handy.

Hole-in-One

Baby likes boards with holes in them. A pegboard with giant pegs (2-in. diameter) can be fun. This is a simple toy to make. Three or four colorful pegs are plenty. Paint with colorful, safe, latex enamel.

"Moo"

Remember the cylindrical noisemaker you had as a child, the one that said "moo" or "meow" when you turned it over? These are still available. Seal one of these in a plastic food storage container so it is safe for Baby to taste. Now that Baby is learning *upside down* and *right-side up,* a picture of a cow glued inside the lid will make playing even more fun and a real learning experience.

Books

Homemade books are special fun and they help Baby learn. They can be picture books of Baby's things—bottles, shoes, cats, dogs, etc. A "people book" with photographs of all the family and friends is also fun. Durable books can be made by covering the pages with clear contact paper or slipping pictures into the plastic photograph holders that come in all sizes.

"Touch and Feel Books" of many textures can include a variety of interesting items such as well-attached bows, buttons, and zippers. These books will provide practice for Baby in the years to come.

"Pat Books" that include noisemakers between the pages so that they squeal when patted are great fun. Inexpensive noisemakers can be purchased at novelty or carnival supply stores. Be sure to attach and conceal them well.

Container Fun

Don't throw away those old boxes, cans, and plastic bottles. The top-of-the-line containers are the great plastic cosmetic cases that are a part of special gift promotions. Clean these containers carefully and let Baby play with them. Different sizes are fun. Big ones are to stick your arm into and retrieve toys. Small ones, which require a finger to coax out the contents, are another favorite. A few interlocking ones and some with lids too big to swallow will provide a challenge for little fingers.

His Own Language

Baby names and calls his friends now:

Mom _____

Dad _____

Siblings _____

Pets _____

His friend _____

Write these names phonetically so that you and others will recognize them. Baby will be delighted that you are finally beginning to decode his language.

Guess Who's Coming to Dinner?

Baby will enjoy being taken to the window to anticipate the homecoming of special people. This is a great learning experience. Be sure that Baby knows the name of the person arriving.

The Crate

A box with the dimensions of a plastic milk crate is a great item to have on hand. For quick cleanup, attach a set of casters and you're ready to roll. Attach a rope and you have a wagon to push, tug, or slide about. Baby will enjoy sharing the crate with his toys. Most of all, Baby will try to get into and out of his crate.

Chorus Time

The timeless song "A-Hunting" can be fun to sing.

A-hunting we will go.
A-hunting we will go.
We'll catch a fox
  (reach for Baby)
And put him in a box
  (bear-hug Baby)
And then we'll let him go
  (sit him down a few inches away).

Make up your own songs, too.

Do You Like My Hat?

Baby will enjoy a hat to plop on his head, especially when he's in front of the mirror. Hang several on a low knob near the mirror, and watch Baby ham it up.

Tickle Times

Tickle games are great fun. Use your hands or Baby's to mime the actions suggested by the words.

Play this tickle game on your squirming baby. He will squeal in anticipatory glee as he becomes familiar with the actions.

Slowly, slowly, very slowly
Creeps the garden snail.
Slowly, slowly, very slowly
Up the wooden rail.
Quickly, quickly, very quickly
Runs the little mouse.
Quickly, quickly, very quickly
Round about the house.

Toes

Baby enjoys playing with his toes. You can make this more fun by playing "Terrific Toes." Baby is beginning to develop a memory, which makes this even more enjoyable.

Terrific Toes

I knows those toes.
I love those toes.
They are a part of me that grows.

Cute and round they touch the ground;
In the air they kick around;
What a sight, and not a sound.

Footprints

If you have been recording Baby's growth periodically, it's time for another footprint.

For contrast, use Baby's white shoe polish on a dark piece of paper. It's amazing to see how much growth has occurred in a few months. Toddlerhood is just around the corner.

A framed series of these prints makes a lovely gift for grandparents or other admirers.

Soapy Magic

Amaze yourself and Baby too by blowing bubbles. A perfect time to practice is bathtime. You need only a bar of soap and your fingers. Curl your index finger and wrap your thumb around it. Rub across a bar of soap. Slowly and gradually release your index finger to form a circle. Blow gently to form a bubble. It is a matter of coordination, determination, and a bit of luck.

"The Sandy Shore"

Now that Baby sits well and loves to crawl, he is ready for some sand play. A sandbox can be a great experience. Pack his favorite measuring cups and bowls, and be off to the park.

You will need to show him the ropes, but soon Baby will master this new environment and look forward to trips to the sand area.

Cut the bottoms off handled plastic milk or juice containers at an angle; these make handy, handled sand scoops. An old big-toothed comb is another fun sand toy.

You can also bring this game to Baby at home. Sprinkle a cup or two of cornmeal in the bottom of a dishpan. Set Baby and the pan on a newspaper-covered floor. Indoor sand play!

Blocks

Cover a half dozen or more 5-in. foam-rubber cubes with cheery fabric for one of Baby's first sets of blocks. This group of toys will be used in many ways. Blocks will be thrown, kicked, gummed, banged, stacked, and carried about.

More High-Chair Art

Instead of chocolate pudding, you can use mashed potato flakes. Sprinkle on Baby's tray. Add a touch of tomato juice (1 tbsp.) and a little warm water. This is tasty fingerpaint for Baby. A good time to use this activity is while you're cooking or busy at the sink.

Touch Board

Baby's busy hands will return again and again to a quick-to-fix, easy-to-change board with a variety of surfaces. Cover a 16 in. x 18 in. piece of corkboard, cardboard, or wood with colored oilcloth or contact paper. Add swatches of material of different textures: sandpaper (scratchy), thick yarn (stringy), etc. Use your imagination. Make sure each item is securely attached.

ROUTINE TIMES

BATHING

Baby's Bath

I'm taking this bath
So I can be
Clean and sweet
And more like me.

A little soap
A little rub
And I will be
Out of this tub.

Then quickly dry
I'll tell you why
I like to smell
. . . just swell.

Tub Time for Two

Baby may enjoy taking his bath with a brother or sister. Trying to get two kids clean at one time means keeping alert . . . and can they splash! Bathwater need only be 3 to 4 inches deep.

Ear Care

Experts tell us that you should not use cotton swabs or anything smaller than your little finger to clean Baby's ears. This is because in trying to remove the wax you might actually force more down into the ear than you remove. The wax can gradually build up and become hard, so that it will have to be removed by a doctor. Washing tiny ears with a little soap and water and a washcloth is all that is necessary and recommended.

Soaps

Let Baby help you at bathtime. Give him some part in this routine. Soap on a rope is one way not to lose the bar, or try a soap that floats.

Toweling It

Do you know Baby's favorite color? Select a terry towel that he will like and indulge his first attempts at drying himself. If given a good example, Baby will, as usual, pick up this technique. This "pat, pat" imitation will delight Baby.

SLEEPING

Bedtime Boss

With so much to see, do, touch, and taste, Baby may not wish to sleep, rest, or even slow down. Bedtimes may become difficult, trying times. Baby's determination to continue even at the end of a busy day is a force to be reckoned with. As the caring adult, it's up to you to set the standards. Decide on a bedtime procedure and, when the lights go out, stick to the plan. Baby needs his rest despite loud, angry, wailing protests to the contrary. Waiting for Baby to signal his desire for sleep could keep you up indefinitely.

Baby's Bedtime Routine

For the world to know, this *is* Baby's routine.

_____

_____

_____

_____

_____

_____

FEEDING

Feeding Himself

Baby has a growing fascination for his spoon. But first, how to use it . . . ah, the problems. Give Baby an opportunity to practice by presenting him with a short-handled wooden spoon. Let him dip the spoon into something stiff or sticky that will adhere to the spoon. Babies have experienced success with mashed potatoes and peanut butter.

Fiddling, Fingers, and Eating

Is Baby finding bananas nice but boring? Now that he has become accomplished with finger foods, a pinch of pizzazz would be appreciated. Try these munchies:

—a little lettuce
—a piece of pear (peeled, please)
—watermelon fingers (without seeds)
—slivers of raw apple
—a waffle finger

Another Feeder

A sibling is often preferred to any other caregiver at mealtime. Somehow it's more fun, or perhaps it's the change of face. A brother or sister who has the time and patience to feed a messy eight-month-old deserves encouragement, watching, and an apron. The social nature of the mealtime banter is usually high kitchen comedy, with Baby initiating much of the conversation.

What I'm Eating

Just so you will have it in writing, complete the following list of what Baby is and is not eating. Caregivers and friends will appreciate it.

	LOVES	HATES
Juices	_____	_____
Cereals (types)	_____	_____
Fruits (strained)	_____	_____
Vegetables	_____	_____
Meats and other proteins	_____	_____
Snacks and finger foods	_____	_____

Very favorite food:

_____

Poorest choice—likely to be refused:

_____

Mixing Your Own

Meats and vegetables are the best buys when it comes to commercially available baby food. Fruit juices and mixed dinners may have a high percentage of fillers and water. Fruit drinks and baby desserts have the lowest food values and are loaded with sugar.

If you like the combination idea, why not mix your own? Choose the meat and vegetable items Baby likes, or ones that you want to introduce.

Open Sez Me

The young mimic loves to imitate faces, especially at mealtime. However, such silliness sometimes keeps him from his food. Don't forget to try these old standbys when facing a baby with a clamped jaw.

Here comes the bee into the hive—buzz buzz buzz
   (aim the spoon toward the mouth)

The airplane is looking for the airport—lay
   out the runway(tongue)—here comes the
   airplane in for a landing.

Here comes the plane into the hangar
   (fly the food into Baby's mouth).

DRESSING AND CHANGING

Cowbell

An eight-month-old who is getting into everything and who is trying to extend his reach so that he may touch untouchables can be hard to keep track of. Attach noisemakers, bells, or clickers to knees, shirts, coveralls, and shoes so that the exploring child will disclose his location with a jingle or two.

Keep Talking

Allow Baby to participate in the dressing process to make this routine more bearable. Remember to chat with the child, "Here is a super red shirt from Aunt Jane with a strawberry on the front . . . over your head it goes. Give me your arm so we can slide it into the sleeve." This is the time to focus on body parts.

Changing Safely

Never take your hand off that baby when it's time for a change. Baby can perform amazing feats of strength while waiting for clean clothes or a dry diaper. Maintain an iron grip and safety will become an automatic part of this routine.

Position

Now that Baby can sit, you may find dressing easiest when he is in a sitting position, rather than trying to dress a squirming Baby determined to practice rolling over. Those with an active baby should consider any strategy that works. Dressing a baby with "things to do" can be a very frustrating experience. Standing may be another position to try.

Suggestions for a Quick Change

These can be invaluable for a sitter or caregiver.

What works _____

_____

_____

What doesn't work _____

_____

_____

Winners (for unexpected reasons) _____

_____

_____

_____

Baby Hats

Babies do not like things that tie under their chins. Hats that do not require ties, such as a knit helmet type, are the best choices. Hooded garments are another alternative.

First Choice

Jogging togs are finally available for infants. These clothes, made in bright, light, stretchy, and durable fabrics, have features that make them favorites with parents. Elasticized ankles keep walkers from tripping over dangling hems, and elasticized wrists keep arms and hands free for action. Most outfits are two-piece and can be layered for warmth. The hooded, zippered jacket is one that babies like.

HELPFUL HINTS

Reminder

Talk to Baby in complete sentences. He is very interested in patterns of speech and will be experimenting with intonation and rhythm patterns.

Incentives

Now that Baby is pulling up to almost any piece of furniture or object that will support his weight, add incentive to his efforts. Give Baby reasons to pull up. Think about rooms he is probably exploring. Plant surprises and treats for the inquisitive child. Position a toy just beyond his grasp on the seat of a chair. Let a portion of a blanket hang over the edge of the couch. Place his Busy Box on the outside edge of his crib so he can pull up to play with the toy.

Too Much Togetherness

Mom and Baby need not (and should not) be together all the time. Both of you deserve occasional rest and time away from each other. These early "time-outs" help Baby begin to handle separations. The first experiences pave the way for handling social situations, sitters, and nursery-school years with greater ease. Understand that no one will ever do everything just as you do. Baby will always have only one mother. However, others can provide him with loving care while you are away.

Baby Food Safety

Remember to check the safety center on the lids of the baby-food jars you buy. The small circle must be concave to ensure that the jar has remained properly vacuum-sealed.

Toughening Togs

Clothes will be expected to withstand extra wear now and in the months to come. Buttons will stay on longer if sewn with durable thread (heavy-duty #8); try using a shank. A small strip of twill tape sewn to the garment before the button is attached will add considerable strength and keep the button from pulling a hole. Buttonholes can be reinforced with heavy-duty thread as well.

Pick, Pick, Pick It Up

Make it a game, but now is the time for Baby to learn to pick up his things. Baby is involved with taking everything out and, with your encouragement, he will soon find putting things back equally fun.

Baby can begin to learn where to find clothes, toys, and other items to play with or wear if they are placed at his level. Graduated wicker baskets are a help.

His Own

A low drawer is a wonderful learning experience for Baby. A challenge to open, to jiggle, to pull and balance, a drawer is something to sit in, put things in, and take things out of. Add a surprise from time to time and keep the explorer happy.

Carpet Safety

It's important to keep your area rugs from sliding and slipping now that Baby is so mobile. Nonslip mats that go under the rug are available for just this purpose. There is also a special double-faced tape that works well with smaller rugs.

Snow Weather

Even though it takes time to bundle up Baby in his snowsuit, do get yourself dressed first. Dressing Baby as quickly as possible will keep him from getting overheated and fussy from the delay. Snowsuits with zippers from neck to toe are the most convenient.

Heating Reminder

Do not warm baby food in the glass jars in which it is purchased; these containers are not heat resistant and could crack. In addition, the unused portion is susceptible to bacteria. Heat in a small saucepan only the amount of food needed. Store the rest in an airtight container in the refrigerator.

Compartments

Baby is a little clutter-creator. Think about a cleanup strategy with a future. Cube-like compartments that can be made or bought commercially can hold and display toys and books now. The units are convenient because they can be stacked or rearranged. In a few years, the cubes can hold puzzles, games, clothes, and gear for the older child.

For a Window Watcher

Next to becoming a master crawler, Baby's favorite activity is looking. Researchers have projected that up to 20 percent of Baby's time is spent viewing objects close at hand. And now Baby is interested in those farther away, too. Baby especially loves to look out of windows—just for the sheer joy of seeing what's out there. Keep windows clean and bright. When cold weather comes, rub salt water or alcohol on the outside of the windows and polish with newspaper.

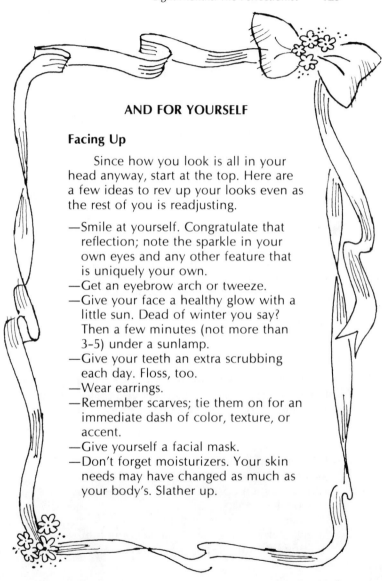

AND FOR YOURSELF

Facing Up

Since how you look is all in your head anyway, start at the top. Here are a few ideas to rev up your looks even as the rest of you is readjusting.

—Smile at yourself. Congratulate that reflection; note the sparkle in your own eyes and any other feature that is uniquely your own.
—Get an eyebrow arch or tweeze.
—Give your face a healthy glow with a little sun. Dead of winter you say? Then a few minutes (not more than 3-5) under a sunlamp.
—Give your teeth an extra scrubbing each day. Floss, too.
—Wear earrings.
—Remember scarves; tie them on for an immediate dash of color, texture, or accent.
—Give yourself a facial mask.
—Don't forget moisturizers. Your skin needs may have changed as much as your body's. Slather up.

Falling, Falling

Baby is into everything. He is testing his body to the upper- and outermost limits. As a result, there may be a temptation to protect him by confining him to a playpen. While this eases your mind, Baby's growth and development can be hampered if he is left alone too long. One solution is to stock up on ice and aspirin. The ice is for the inevitable bumps and bruises; the aspirin for your predictable headache. Be prepared to console and cuddle.

Spotless

Some people *do* think of everything! One mom uses furniture casters on the four corners of the playpen when she takes it outdoors. This neat housekeeper reports that bringing mud, dirt, and grime inside is no longer a problem because of this simple measure.

The Beach Baby

Why exclude Baby from a trip to the shore? He will have a happy time and so will you by following these suggestions offered by beachcombing parents:

—Take several jugs of water for drinking, rinsing off, and keeping cool
—Take or rent an umbrella; Baby is especially sensitive to sun
—Turn a playpen upside down for a safe, protected play or sleep space
—Circular, portable, expandable gates are a nifty way to give Baby play space while keeping him from dashing into the ocean

Rocker

There is no place like a rocking chair for comforting and cuddling. Keep the chair in operation and the floor beneath it in good repair by protecting rocker arcs with adhesive tape or felt dots (the kind used on the bottom of lamps).

Telephone Tip

The phone rings or a call must be made. Try spaghetti, wet or dry, to keep Baby busy and happy while you converse.

Dry: Two or three strands of spaghetti or noodles will respond to the grasp of a young child by breaking, snapping, and popping. Baby will be intrigued by trying to pick up the little pieces.

Wet: A cooked noodle or two of any width will wiggle about on Baby's feeding tray. A noodle can slip, slide, swirl, and be chased by little fingers. It tastes good, too.

Super Swing

One creative father we know quickly made a supersafe swing out of an infant car seat. He hung the well-designed, padded, and belted seat from the limb of an apple tree. His baby enjoyed the swing all summer long.

No Mud

We were walking after a rain one day and noticed a baby carriage with wheel covers coming towards us. Always on the alert for helpful hints, we stopped and asked about them. The woman told us that they were just plastic bowl covers (they look like little shower hats) she puts on the carriage when it's wet and muddy outside. She can slip the covers off when she gets home without having to worry about tracking mud into the house.

Hat Trick

A quick way to shape and dry Baby's hats and caps is to place them on an inflated balloon. They'll soon be restored to their original size.

Instant Boots

For added protection in inclement weather, reach for two plastic bags or several sheets of clear food wrap to cover Baby's shoes. Secure these instant boots with rubber bands or shoelaces. In an emergency, these boots will also work for adults.

Ten-Minute Blitz

Setting a kitchen timer for ten minutes when cleaning a part of your home out of baby's sight has become an absolute necessity. This blitz technique allows you to concentrate all your energies for short periods of time. We have found that this method also soothes the conscience. You will discover that a lot can be accomplished in these short periods.

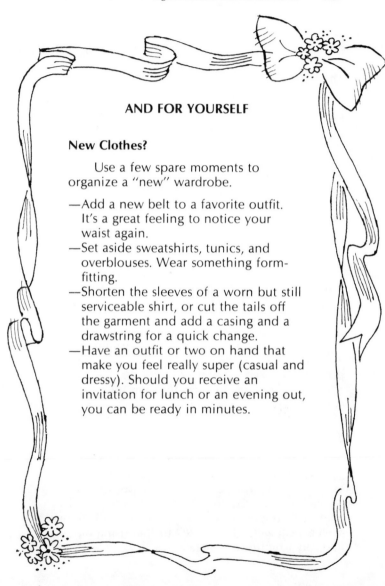

AND FOR YOURSELF

New Clothes?

Use a few spare moments to organize a "new" wardrobe.

—Add a new belt to a favorite outfit. It's a great feeling to notice your waist again.
—Set aside sweatshirts, tunics, and overblouses. Wear something form-fitting.
—Shorten the sleeves of a worn but still serviceable shirt, or cut the tails off the garment and add a casing and a drawstring for a quick change.
—Have an outfit or two on hand that make you feel really super (casual and dressy). Should you receive an invitation for lunch or an evening out, you can be ready in minutes.

PARENTS, FRIENDS, AND ADMIRERS

The Human Chair

We recently spotted a very delighted baby having a splendid ride in an instant apparatus created by a "special male friend." The baby's chair was made by clasping the friend's hands together and arranging the rider so that his back was supported against his friend's chest. The infant's feet looped over the top of the friend's arms. Security and closeness were created by drawing the friend's arms in toward his own chest.

Toys Are for Babies

Yesterday's toys may be totally forgotten for now. The cruising eight-month-old may forgo all objects save those that share his crib. If he chooses any favorite items, they are most likely ones that are of use to you—pots, pans, utensils. Share your wealth with Baby . . . or buy a second just for him. Those measuring spoons, cups, utensils, bowls, and small pots will be used for sand toys, for playing house, and for other dramatic adventures in the months to come.

Chipless Dip

When planning a get-together for friends, consider Baby, too. Before you add spices or other exotic items to your dip, take out a portion for Baby. A touch of food coloring will catch his eye. Baby may try to use his treat like the big folks or he may prefer his finger. Mothers tell us that using dip is a fine way to introduce vegetables.

Saving Memories

Take the time to jot down several of Baby's latest antics. These prized memories will be appreciated later. So record them now.

_____

_____

_____

_____

_____

_____

_____

Guests

Visitors may be surprised by Baby's response to their presence. At this age, Baby will need additional assistance and attention in order to respond easily to company. This social shyness is typical of nearly all infants of this age. Kind words, hugging, and information about the guests will make a difference. Let Baby make the first move. He will let you know when he is ready to be held or handled by others.

Away

Prepare Baby in advance for times away from home. Verbal reassurance helps. So does taking familiar toys and one special surprise. Move slowly.

Spend time talking to Baby and prepare him for new experiences. This will be rewarding.

Mountain-Climber

Baby will enjoy the adventure of climbing a human mountain. Have one of Baby's bigger admirers spread out on the floor and let Baby enjoy the closeness and challenge of crawling over this special friend. This is a good motor-development game for Baby.

Tapes

Remember the archive. Tape a sample of the talking baby who may be putting syllables together: *dada, mama,* etc. These recordings will be savored now and become a source of amusement later.

Snapshots

How about a family photo while you're capturing special moments?

Funny Face

A cookie that looks good and tastes even better could have a face like Baby's. This fun-to-frost-and-create treat might be made by an older sibling or young friend. Decorate a plain, nonsweet cookie with a touch of icing and draw a face.

Soft Sculpture or Pillow Plus

While primarily interested in climbing and cruising about, Baby will still opt for a comfy place in which to curl up. Make a tomato, a cushiony doughnut, a naugahyde cucumber, or a fluffy cloud to roll over. Consider including handles or crawl-through spaces in these material sculptures. Baby will climb over, lean against, and explore this form, which will be the site of many games for years to come.

For the less creative, attach three or four pillows of odd or standard sizes to make a "magic mass." This challenging terrain will help the child practice motor skills as it becomes a favorite lounging spot in the future.

A friend who made a pillow plus for her baby found that it was still being used by her teenager.

Gifts

An Activity Box is a great present for Baby. The best boxes have things to push, pull, poke, and turn. All parts of this box should make noises. Best of all, nothing comes off, so no cleanup. Baby will continue to enjoy this toy until he is two or so.

A homemade busy box with a variety of things to try, touch, turn, and test is indeed a special gift. Items to include in your design:

—a caster with a wheel to spin
—a lock with a permanently attached key to twist back and forth
—a bell to ring
—a handle to turn
—a bicycle horn (bulb type) to poke or squeeze

—a latch to lift
—a chain to rattle
—a bolt to throw

Consider any hardware-store item that moves, emits sound, pushes or pulls, slides, or rolls.

Beads

One of our favorite grandmothers from the Midwest regularly makes "bread beads" for her favorite baby. First, she reserves some bread dough and molds it into interesting shapes. After poking a large hole in each bead, she allows the beads to rise, and then bakes them. For a finishing touch, she likes to glaze them with a little egg white and water.

She strings four or five of these shiny shapes on a thick cotton cord or yarn. This easy-to-make gift is fun to wear and is a fine teething toy.

For a slightly older sibling, the baker made a lovely tinted heart to wear and nibble. Both items were designed and intended for immediate consumption.

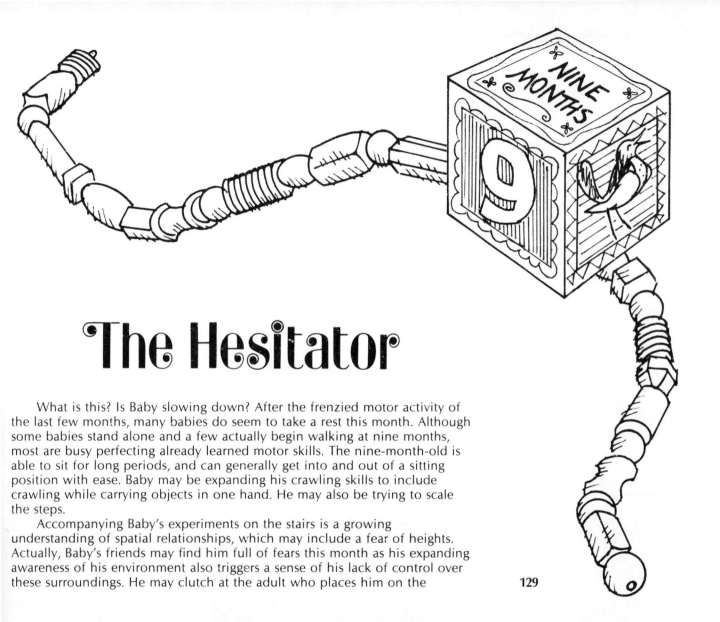

The Hesitator

What is this? Is Baby slowing down? After the frenzied motor activity of the last few months, many babies do seem to take a rest this month. Although some babies stand alone and a few actually begin walking at nine months, most are busy perfecting already learned motor skills. The nine-month-old is able to sit for long periods, and can generally get into and out of a sitting position with ease. Baby may be expanding his crawling skills to include crawling while carrying objects in one hand. He may also be trying to scale the steps.

Accompanying Baby's experiments on the stairs is a growing understanding of spatial relationships, which may include a fear of heights. Actually, Baby's friends may find him full of fears this month as his expanding awareness of his environment also triggers a sense of his lack of control over these surroundings. He may clutch at the adult who places him on the

129

changing table or in the tub. He may react with tears to loud noises. These events are all part of Baby's growth; with a little time and sympathy his fears will subside.

Baby is making cognitive leaps this month. His growing understanding of spatial relationships and his greater dexterity give him the ability to build towers out of two or three objects. His memory is developing rapidly; he searches for objects that have been removed from his sight and recalls recent events and routines. For example, if his daily bath follows dinner, Baby will let you know that he expects this.

You may hear Baby imitating noises as well as words this month. He is learning to cough, click, make airplane sounds, etc., deliberately. He will also be practicing his words, sometimes in long sequences such as *da-da-da-da-da-da-da*. Some babies can respond to verbal commands during the ninth month and will comply with great satisfaction to a simple request such as "Pick up your bottle, Josh."

ACTIVITIES, GAMES, AND SONGS

Ring Toys

Give Baby a spindle toy with which to play. With your help and encouragement, Baby will learn to put the rings on the spindle. Once he has learned this, he will practice again and again with great satisfaction.

Spindle toys are easy to make. Use your imagination. A hand with a big thumb to ring, a stuffed teapot, or a pumpkin with a big stem would all appeal to Baby. Use doughnut shapes cut from wood and pad them thoroughly with stuffing. Now make a fabric cover for your creation.

Clapping Song

Baby especially enjoys hand clapping. Play this little clapping song as the words suggest (to the tune of "Little Brown Jug"):

Clap your hands, one, two, three,
Play a little game with me.
Now your hands have flown away.
Come back hands so we can play.

Help Baby clap his hands and then hide them behind his back. As Baby learns the song, he can do more and more by himself. He will also like being the one to initiate this game.

Balloons

Baby will enjoy kicking, pulling, and chasing a fast-moving balloon on a string.

Strutting

During this month and until Baby is walking independently, his favorite game will be walking and stomping his feet while you hold his hands. Baby needs this motor practice, so play often.

String-along

Baby is learning to use tools. String toys are a fascination as he learns that pulling the string will fetch the toy. These fun-to-make toys are great gifts. You can assemble impromptu toys from an assortment of other toys and gadgets or make them from scratch. The important thing is to include moving parts that will make noises when moved—measuring spoons, wooden spools, blocks, plastic bangle bracelets, keys, etc.

Collage

Pasting a collage of colorful scraps of paper, fabric, and trim can be fun for Baby. Tape a piece of colored paper to his high-chair tray that will contrast with the scraps.

Dribble a trail of white nontoxic glue around the paper. Next show Baby how to push the scraps onto the dribbles of glue. Now stand back and let the artist create.

These artistic creations can be mounted in a clear plastic block frame and given to an admiring grandparent or friend, or they can brighten Baby's own room.

The Cat Says "Meow"

Baby is alert to all sorts of environmental noises and tries to imitate them. Animal sounds and pictures hold special interest.

Naming the animals and imitating the sounds they make will provide beneficial early experiences with beginning books. Encourage Baby to actively participate by pointing and imitating.

Such songs as "Old MacDonald Had a Farm" have not lost their popularity with young children. Many of the songs sung to a child at an early age will give special pleasure when he learns to sing them himself. This can be a fun family game, especially for young brothers and sisters.

At Last

Baby can at long last retrieve toys that are tied to his high chair or walker. This is a sign of beginning problem solving, and Baby enjoys practicing this new accomplishment.

76 Trombones

Musical instruments provide exciting experiences for Baby. Bells, tambourines, and sand blocks can be purchased or easily made. In order to make sand blocks, cover several wooden blocks with sandpaper and use a small drawer knob for a handle. A tambourine can be made by lacing two aluminum pie pans together with a string of jingle bells so that the bells are around the edges. Baby will enjoy playing along with a song like John Philip Sousa's "Stars and Stripes Forever."

All in a Row

Wooden clothespins are great baby toys. Just dumping them from their bag is a lark. And there are many other great games that can be played with clothespins.

Line them up on the edge of a loaf pan and let Baby take them off and drop them into the pan.

A plastic container can be combined with the pins for a great game of "Dropping In and Shaking Out." Hard work for Baby, but what satisfaction.

Catchall

By now there are lots of odd pieces of games that no longer exist among Baby's toys. These odds and ends can be stored in a dump can, solely intended, as the name implies, for dumping. Baby will enjoy emptying and filling this container of goodies. A large plastic food container makes a great "dumper," but any container will do. Add a few new treasures such as fabric squares, junk mail, and a ring box with a little cereal inside to reward Baby's thoroughness.

Snap, Pop

If you have more money than time, giant plastic pop beads are an inexpensive learning toy for Baby. They make great necklaces, bracelets, and crowns.

Plumber's Special

An eight-to-ten-inch section of clear plastic hose (3-in. diameter) or pipe with edges that have been smoothed can be a versatile baby toy. Show Baby how to drop small objects through the pipe so he can watch them fall. Try whispering through the pipe or blowing gently.

Buy extras for the bath and beach.

Sock Bottle

Cut a medium-sized plastic bottle about 6 inches from the bottom. Now, using the bottom half, pull an old sock up over the bottle's bottom. What you have is a safe, intriguing toy for Baby, a mystery bottle. Fill the bottle with several of Baby's small toys—blocks, rattles, or jingle bells on an elastic wristband. Show Baby how to put his hand into the bottle and pull out a treasure.

Not Too Young

Baby is not too young to enjoy coloring with felt tip markers (nontoxic and nonpermanent color) or crayons. If possible, use slick finish paper; it will make the most of his marking efforts. He will need your help at first to get the idea of marking, but will be excited to see the results of these efforts.

Painting

Your baby will enjoy painting with stubby half-inch pastry brushes. A little chocolate pudding, colored whipped topping, or tomato sauce will make a great paint. A roll of masking tape can be used to attach a small pot-pie paint pan to Baby's high-chair tray.

Watching the World

Babies enjoy looking out of the window. If you have glass patio doors, Baby can safely look out while he is in his walker or jump seat. Placing Baby securely in his high chair in front of a window will also allow him to visually explore his neighborhood between outings.

Talk Time

Baby is just beginning to discover a new toy, the telephone. By playing the telephone game, Baby gets the idea of conversation.

Toy telephones are inexpensive and can provide hours of fun. Help Baby by playing "Hello" together.

Once Baby becomes interested in phones, remember to keep the real phone out of reach. It may end up off the hook if you don't.

Rag Bag

A basket of cloth scraps of various textures and colors will surely be scattered all over the room, but Baby will have great fun with them. Add several features and little bits of yarn, too.

Take Time

Take the time now to record some of your favorite anecdotes about Baby. There are only a few months left before Baby will enter his toddler years.

_____

_____

_____

_____

_____

_____

Just the Right Size

Baby is becoming a climber and trying to get into or on everything. He will enjoy being able to climb into a low child's chair. One of the safest types is a molded plastic cube chair. These versatile cubes come in sets of three. Depending on which surface is up, the cube is a very low chair, a slightly higher chair, or a table. The three together make a colorful table and chairs that Baby can use now and throughout his preschool years. They are sold at educational supply stores.

Stairs

Baby is ready and interested in practicing going upstairs. Stairs are a developmental challenge for Baby. The safest way to provide this experience is with his own set of two or three low steps that he can safely negotiate.

Anyone handy with tools can build a set, or you can make them from cardboard boxes that have been weighted by filling with newspapers. The steps can be covered with colorful contact paper or vinyl wallpaper. They will provide Baby with safe climbing practice.

Here's a Ball

Here's a finger play for Baby. Just use your fingers to make balls of graduated size as you say the simple words and count. The first ball is formed with thumb and index finger, the second ball with two hands, and the third ball by both arms. Help Baby make the movements, too.

Here's a ball,
and here's a ball,
and here's a great big ball!
Let's count them,
One, two, three.

Roll the Ball

Simple but fun, roll a ball to Baby. He will enjoy sitting straddle-legged across from you as you roll the ball back and forth. Brothers and sisters can enjoy this game, too. Knowing that Baby likes playing ball may be quite reassuring to them. Maybe Baby's not so bad after all.

ROUTINE TIMES

BATHING

Reminder

While dressing or bathing Baby, sing some of the tunes or play the games (see "Activities, Games, and Songs") that develop an interest in body parts. Baby will play a real role in these games now and may try to say the words or indicate that he knows what you mean if you give him the opportunity.

Bathtime Safety

Never, never leave Baby alone in the bathtub. While he may look peaceful and content, bathtime is the time to give him your complete attention. Even in only several inches of water, there is real danger.

A rubber bath mat is a good safety precaution. It is reassuring to Baby since its texture is less slippery than the tub's.

Hanging On

Some babies experience temporary fear of the tub at nine months. A time or two in the tub with you might help. An old pair of cotton work gloves will improve your grip.

More Practice

The tub is a fine place to practice handling a cup. Drinking bathwater is not a serious offense, and mess is of little or no concern. Drinking from a cup is still a game. Provide the essential link by bringing Baby's favorite cup to the tub.

SLEEPING

Bedtime Buddy

A small unbreakable mirror attached to Baby's crib where he can see himself can give you a few extra minutes of shut-eye. If a mirror is already part of the crib, move it to a new location and watch Baby amuse himself anew.

Baby's Nap

An important part of successfully bedding Baby down for his nap is establishing a routine and sticking to it. The routine need not be unpleasant, but it must be consistent. Here is a little poem to say as you lay Baby down, cover him, and then snuggle and pat his back a few moments until he falls asleep. This helps Baby know what to expect.

Here's our Baby ready for his nap,
Lay him down in his mother's lap;
Cover him up so he won't peep,
Rock him till he's fast asleep.

FEEDING

Enough Is Enough

Feeding reminder—babies will truly eat only what they need to eat and no more. Unless you, the caregiver, force him to continue, Baby will stop. Yes, you can overfeed Baby! So be alert to his signals. An additional snack or a minimeal is a nutritionally sound and efficient alternative to three big meals.

A Tea Party

Baby will probably develop his cup-drinking skills this month. Fun and learning occur when your little imitator has a tea party with an older sibling. Baby will watch the child use a cup and will copy the action, especially if the beverage is delicious.

Me First

Feeding Baby first can save all members of the family from a lot of frustration. That Baby has very little patience is an understatement. By starting his meal with a few things he can eat independently, the rest of the family may get started before he requires more attention.

Reminder

Do remember to use some of the suggestions from earlier months about ways to secure Baby's dish to his tray when he is practicing his emerging spoon skills, lest you have a disaster.

Spoons

Now that Baby is beginning to use a spoon, there are many special ones from which to select. Most mothers seem to prefer small metal spoons or baby-sized spoons. Spoons with special coatings that are easy on tender gums are nice, too.

Plastic spoons will not work as Baby has more crunch to his bite than you think and may break them.

Bowls

A large plastic soup bowl with sloping sides is the best serving dish for Baby. Its sides allow food to be cornered and forced onto the spoon.

Brown Bag Delight

When fixing Baby's lunches to be eaten away from home, keep portions small, tasty, colorful, and easy to eat. Baby can feed himself better these days.

Many of the best ideas will be inspired by those good hors d'oeuvres sampled at Mom's and Dad's last get-together. Many of these goodies can be made up ahead of time and frozen. Thus lunch can be assembled quickly and will be thawed at room temperature when it's time to eat.

Suggestions for easy lunches include:

Fruit
Applesauce
Fruit cup (your own or canned)
Seedless tangerines
Mandarin orange slices
Banana disks

Vegetables (blanch lightly so still firm, but not impossibly hard)
Carrots and zucchini sticks spread with peanut butter
Broccoli/cauliflower flowerets with a dip
Cherry tomatoes stuffed with cream cheese

Bread and Crackers
Cheese crackers
Toast in fancy shapes (buttered, please)

Bagel in bite-sized pieces
Pita bread cut into wedges
Graham crackers
Animal crackers
Wheat crackers (make your own and add wheat
   germ, cheese, and parsley)
Croutons; for dessert add honey or cinnamon

Miscellaneous
Yogurt with fruit
Cottage cheese with mixed vegetables
Dab of egg salad
Bits of cooked chicken or shrimp
Fingers or chunks of cheese
Spinach balls made with stuffing mix
Peas
Cold rice salad
Peanut butter balls
Cheese puffs
Tapioca pudding
Grated carrot and fruit salad
Thick cereal; oatmeal or farina with fruit and yogurt
Melted cheese sandwiches, open-faced

DRESSING AND CHANGING

Diapering

Some babies may begin to fight you if you try to diaper them lying down. So try the procedure with Baby standing up, holding onto your shoulders. If possible, allow Baby to hand you the diaper and tell him what you are doing and why.

Mother's Little Helper

If Baby is not already helping you, why not encourage him to remove certain items of clothing, but only when you are ready. He can certainly manage shoes, once untied, and probably socks.

Shoes and Socks

Baby can now take off his shoes and often his socks. Sometimes it's important to keep them on. Save the exasperation and double knot! You can also buy bells and infant shoe "barrels" that will serve this purpose.

Shoe Business

Now that Baby is cruising or beginning to take a few steps, try some of these suggestions about his shoes:

—Remember to have Baby try on both shoes with socks that are the correct size. Recheck the fit after four to six weeks; feet grow fast.
—To keep shoes shiny after polishing, paint several thin layers of shellac over the tips. This treatment will protect shoes from nicks and scratches.

Socks Up!

If your baby is walking, he is probably wearing shoes and, of course, socks. To keep those socks from sliding down his ankle and disappearing altogether, place a strip of adhesive tape inside the shoe above the heel.

HELPFUL HINTS

Reminder

If Baby seems uninterested in his toys and other activities, be patient. He is concentrating all his energy on developing his new mobility skills. He may be crawling, cruising, pulling up, or walking, but, regardless of his style, Baby is working hard.

Table Tips

Baby has discovered that he can get many things by pulling. Baby can get himself up and he can bring things down to have a look. With this in mind, rethink the tables and ledges in your home. Beware the fringe or attractive tablecloth edge; be aware of tassels on the end of a runner. For now, it may be best to reposition coverings or to remove them altogether.

Gates

With Baby's cruising, pulling up, and exploring, now is the time to evaluate living and playing sites in the environment in order to determine to which areas you wish to limit him. Are there any areas you want to close off? Someone handy with tools can make a simple gate out of plywood. Such gates are desirable because Baby cannot see further than the top of the barrier. Lattice-type gates are to be avoided, as we have known many a bright, ingenious baby who has learned to climb over by gaining a toehold and vaulting over. A sturdy gate with baby-proofed latches can maximize your child's safety and security and minimize your anxiety.

Diet Planning

As you plan Baby's diet, keep in mind that fruits and fruit juices tend to soften stools. Prunes, apricots, and peaches help to prevent constipation when homogenized milk is introduced. Cheese, milk, highly processed breads, and cereals tend to firm stools. Vegetables and whole grains add needed roughage and bulk. Adequate fluids, including water, are important items in any child's diet.

Out Spot!

Oops! Baby's diaper has leaked on the rug! This common accident needs to be dealt with as quickly as possible. The high alkaline concentration can change the color of the carpet. Be prepared with a premixed solution and a clean sponge.

First, using lukewarm water, sponge the area several times. Blot up as much moisture as possible with a second clean sponge or cloth.

Next, apply a mixture of 1 tsp. white vinegar and 2 tsp. lukewarm water. With a medicine dropper, saturate the spot using a circular motion. Allow the solution to remain on the stain for 15 minutes. Blot up excess solution. Sponge area several times with lukewarm water. The last sponging should follow the direction of the pile. Allow to dry completely.

Emergency Closing

To discourage curious fingers, seal a lower cupboard in a new room or at a friend's home quickly with a short piece of strapping tape.

Bent Out of Shape

Are rubber and plastic toys looking a bit worn and misshapen? Improve their form by dipping them in very hot water for a few minutes. Then restore them to their original proportions.

While at this task, see the suggestions for cleaning plastics.

Keep Plastic Fantastic

Many of Baby's utensils will be made of plastic. Durable as these items can be, they tend to need periodic sprucing up. To keep bottles, bowls, and containers looking fresh, use liquid cleansers that have the kind of mildness yet effectiveness to do a good job on the smoothest surfaces.

Textured plastic responds well to a light sprinkling of cleanser or a hand soap containing pumice particles. Scrub well with a knitted plastic mesh sponge to avoid additional scratches.

Brown Bagging It

For the baby who eats away from home—at a sitter's, day care, or with friends—pack his lunch in one of these unusual ways:

—a backpack/duffel bag
—an artist box (many are plastic)
—a tour pack (check bike shops)
—the classic fisherman's bag with leather fasteners (check sporting goods stores)
—a wicker hamper, perhaps a rectangular or Chinese "wedding" basket (circular shape); line these with vinyl for added durability

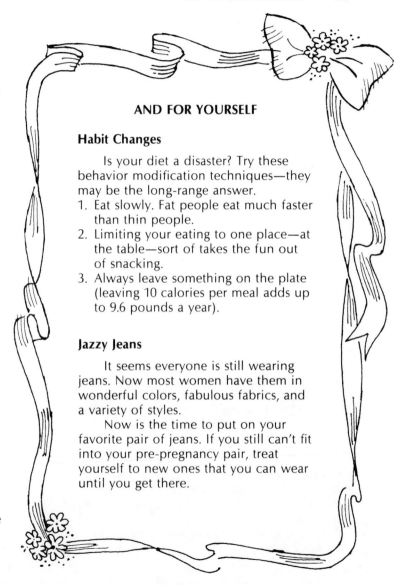

AND FOR YOURSELF

Habit Changes

Is your diet a disaster? Try these behavior modification techniques—they may be the long-range answer.
1. Eat slowly. Fat people eat much faster than thin people.
2. Limiting your eating to one place—at the table—sort of takes the fun out of snacking.
3. Always leave something on the plate (leaving 10 calories per meal adds up to 9.6 pounds a year).

Jazzy Jeans

It seems everyone is still wearing jeans. Now most women have them in wonderful colors, fabulous fabrics, and a variety of styles.

Now is the time to put on your favorite pair of jeans. If you still can't fit into your pre-pregnancy pair, treat yourself to new ones that you can wear until you get there.

Remember that most of these containers will hold bottles, jars, and plastic bags. They need to be flexible and sturdy at the same time.

Make certain that these "lunch boxes" can be hung or left flat. In warmer weather, an insulated container is probably a good idea. And remember a label with Baby's name and phone number.

That's Mine

Nothing is more frustrating than discovering that Baby and his possessions have become separated while he has been away. Increase the chances of keeping what's rightfully his. It's not too soon to order special name tags for a baby who is away from home. These printed cloth tags can be ordered from stationery stores. Perhaps a stencil with his initials can be applied to his paraphernalia. For the patient parent, an embroidered trademark is nice; a bunny, sun, or strawberry are easily identifiable.

Code System for the Lunch Box Set

Whenever more than two babies get together, the equipment begins to look amazingly alike. To keep confusion to a minimum, may we suggest the following ideas for marking bottles, jars, lunch boxes, and containers that will be washed daily and subjected to the hardest sort of use.

—A ring of several strips of colored plastic tape. Choose a color scheme; tricolors are pleasing.
—An indelible laundry marker
—Nail polish (avoid frosted hues); the brush can do whatever you like
—A kit for marking sporting equipment works well on baby gear

—A stencil with small letters (from the hobby shop)
—A family insignia (think of what some famous designers have done with initials)

Soft Parts

Toss a stiffened pair of plastic pants into the dryer with a batch of towels to soften them. Or, add a little baby oil to the final rinse to keep the plastic from cracking and stiffening.

Leave-taking

Baby has become a careful observer with a memory. Based on clues he has picked up, he can predict when you might leave the house. So, do not attempt to sneak out. It is far better to deal with a few tears and explain your departure than to alarm him by having him suddenly discover that you have already gone.

Keep Calling

Baby is a getaway artist. His movements have grown refined. He can turn on a dime and scurry away. Keep in touch by constant calling. Make this a routine game and insist on a response. Immediately track down a player who stops returning a call.

Spotless Socks

To get the socks of a busy baby clean, try:

—Soaking socks in a solution of washing soda and warm water for 30 minutes before washing
—Boiling white cotton socks briefly in water with a tablespoonful of cream of tartar before washing
—Adding a bit of borax to the wash

PARENTS, FRIENDS, AND ADMIRERS

Jack-in-the-Box

Baby will be captivated by a jack-in-the-box. He will soon learn to anticipate the appearance of Jack. Turning the handle of a musical box will add to his fun.

Remember:

Jack-in-the-box,
You sit so still.
Won't you come out?
Sure I will.

This is also a favorite action song for young children. Hold Baby with his feet on the floor in a partial squat as you recite the poem. Ask Baby to come out and then help him spring from his position. Later he can play this exciting game alone.

Boats

A brother or sister might enjoy making a boat for himself or herself and one for Baby, too. These easy-to-assemble toys start with a milk carton, or a small, 4-oz. juice carton or whipping-cream container. To assemble:

1. Wash carton and dry thoroughly.
2. Close top, staple or tape shut.
3. Add smokestacks, sails, and portholes. Use pieces of paper straw for the smokestacks and masts.
4. Decorate with colored plastic tape.
5. Sail in or out of the tub.

These boats could become the first portion of a flotilla—all child-designed and created.

Block Covers

One of the greatest dimestore discoveries we've made lately is paper block covers in an inexpensive cutout book. These paper covers—trucks, cars, buildings, etc.—are designed to be used over a variety of empty paper milk cartons. They make a delightful set of blocks.

The nonartistic admirer who wants to make a special gift should keep these in mind. Clear contact paper will make these beauties last.

Baby's Phone List

By now you've discovered that Baby prefers the company of other babies, perhaps to the exclusion of all other people, toys, or routines. So, make a list of Baby's favorites and invite a friend over soon.

NAME	PHONE NUMBER
_____	_____
_____	_____
_____	_____

A Day Outside

An opportunity for a splendid day begins with a lightweight stroller. Take a blanket, pack a light snack for a picnic, and off to the great outdoors.

Your strutting baby will revel in the textures, sights, and sounds of the outdoor world. No matter what the weather, you and Baby will have an exciting, easy day.

Visiting Safely

If Baby will be coming to stay for a week or more, remain his faithful admirer by preparing your home and yourself in the following ways:

—Put all breakables out of reach
—Remove all lightweight furniture
—Cover electrical outlets with tape as a temporary measure
—Beware of all sockets and cords; move as necessary or reposition
—Limit the number of rooms Baby will frequent
—Select a variety of small items from your kitchen and put them in a basket or box ready for use when Baby gets bored
—Have a card table ready to use as an instant gate (to block off a stairway, etc.); place a heavy chair behind the table
—Make a note of the phone number of a trusted baby-sitter so that you and Baby's parents can arrange a night out

These measures will be greatly appreciated by Baby and will allow you to show your hospitality and concern in practical ways.

Baby Photography

Babies and children are the most photographed of all subjects. Successful child photography involves nothing more than capturing on film the spirit of childhood. Infant pictures often have this quality because babies are not as aware of the camera as older children; they're not as easily distracted.

Don't try to direct the action, rather capture the child involved in the activity of his choice. Picture series showing complete stories can be especially effective. Since most babies repeat enjoyable activities, the opportunities to snap the action are ample.

Lower the level of your camera so that it is even with the child's eyes, giving you Baby's perspective of the world.

Needlework

A piece of needlepoint that captures faithfully one of Baby's artworks can be a gift of love. This can easily be done by reproducing the artwork on the needlepoint canvas with acrylic paint after tracing the outline onto it with carbon paper. Maybe not the professional way, but it works. This can also be done with embroidery.

These masterpieces could also be reproduced onto your favorite child's clothing.

Picture Books

Colorful picture books such as *The Three Little Kittens* or *Animals and Their Babies* are good beginning storybooks for Baby. These books, made of sturdy, wipeable cardboard, are welcome gifts that a friend can send across the miles to surprise Baby and his family.

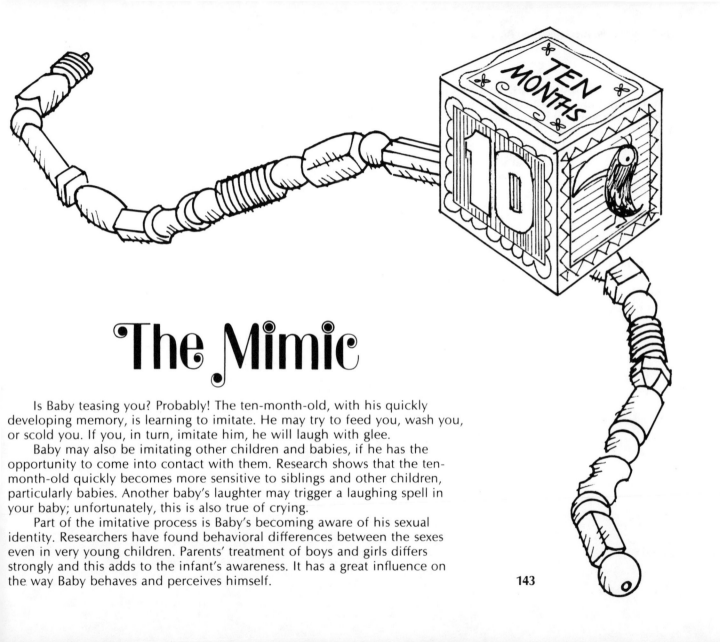

The Mimic

Is Baby teasing you? Probably! The ten-month-old, with his quickly developing memory, is learning to imitate. He may try to feed you, wash you, or scold you. If you, in turn, imitate him, he will laugh with glee.

Baby may also be imitating other children and babies, if he has the opportunity to come into contact with them. Research shows that the ten-month-old quickly becomes more sensitive to siblings and other children, particularly babies. Another baby's laughter may trigger a laughing spell in your baby; unfortunately, this is also true of crying.

Part of the imitative process is Baby's becoming aware of his sexual identity. Researchers have found behavioral differences between the sexes even in very young children. Parents' treatment of boys and girls differs strongly and this adds to the infant's awareness. It has a great influence on the way Baby behaves and perceives himself.

143

Baby's fine-motor skills are developing noticeably this month. Although you may not always notice it, Baby is distinguishing between what he does with his left and right hands. The hand he uses for sucking is often his passive hand; he leaves the other free for exploring and manipulating. And explore he does, particularly with his index finger. He is interested in probing and poking everything, and is particularly delighted when he can insert his finger into something. Now it becomes especially important to cover plugs and sockets, and to remove from harm's way any utensils, etc., that might cause an injury.

Baby is adding gestures to his words. He may wave "bye-bye," shake his head "no," or smack his lips to "eat." Sometimes these words and gestures are practiced to the extent that they lose their practical meaning and become a nonsense game for Baby.

Although Baby's ninth month motor lull will probably continue, he may begin "cruising." This is when Baby walks along the furniture, steadying himself with a hand-over-hand procedure. Some babies develop this preliminary to walking, others don't.

ACTIVITIES, GAMES, AND SONGS

A Ball for Baby

This month baby will enjoy playing with a clear plastic ball with moving objects inside. Baby will be interested in this object-within-an-object concept.

Music Magic

Now that Baby has the idea that strings are to pull, he will enjoy an assortment of musical toys that "talk" when their strings are pulled. He will enjoy most pull toys that make a noise.

Fit Togethers

Look around the house for the interlocking things that might make safe stacking toys for Baby. He is very interested in putting things inside each other. Measuring cups are the most obvious, but certainly not the only, household items that can be used this way. Anything that is safe and comes in graduated sizes will delight Baby.

Baby Toss

Baby is learning to throw. A variety of colorful beanbags can make throwing great fun. Since Baby is aware of differences in texture, fill the bags with several different materials—split peas, lima beans, macaroni, navy beans, etc. This will give Baby things to compare and problems to solve. You might slip in a bell or two as a surprise.

Make sure that the beans are securely inside and will stay there. A double lining is a good precaution.

Bags can be made up in a variety of shapes, from a simple square to a frog.

Having something into which to throw the bags makes this game more fun. Depending on the time you want to spend, let Baby toss the bags into a wastebasket or onto a homemade beanbag toss face.

Let Me Get to It!

Remember the storage ideas from earlier chapters? As you start to rearrange Baby's things so he can take a more active role, consider recycling the ideas for toy storage. Arrange his toys so that he has access to them.

A "Sit In"

The rubber tub that came with your changing table or that you used for Baby's first baths can become a favorite toy. Baby will enjoy climbing in and out of it, or filling it with toys and then dumping them out. A plastic milk crate is also great fun, as is a cardboard box.

Roll the Ball

Rolling balls back and forth is a favorite game at this age. This is a great way for older brothers and sisters to play with Baby. It is also a good group game for several babies.

Hiding Game

Now that Baby knows that objects have permanence, that they exist even when they are not in view, hiding games have taken on new meaning. Baby will search with new determination for the hidden toy. Baby rarely tires of hide-and-seek. There are endless variations—hide the toy, you hide, Baby hides, etc. All are fun.

Building

Baby is beginning to learn about tower building. It's time to bring out blocks of heavy cardboard or wood instead of the cloth ones. The latter can still be used for throwing and squeezing.

At first, Baby will need to watch you and others to get the idea of building, but, as we all know, he is a great mimic. Soon building will come into its own.

Let's Try It Again

It's time to review some of the songs and finger games you've been playing. Baby can now take an active part. Remember "Just Like Me," from Chapter 5? Now Baby can initiate the game and you follow. Or how about "Pat-a-Cake," (Chapter 7). Here is a new one. It involves a little more activity but is sure to become a favorite.

CUP OF TEA

Here's a cup
　(form cup with one hand),
And here's a cup
　(form cup with other hand),
And here's a pot of tea
　(form teapot with both hands).
Pour a cup
　(pouring motion),
And pour a cup
　(pouring motion),
And have a drink with me
　(pretend to drink).

Squat and Jump

Baby's interest in his new upright position and in a sense of movement makes this game special fun. Hold Baby under the arms while he is standing on a table or chair. Show him how to relax and bend his knees as you say "squat." Then, when you say "jump," help him jump. This can be played until your arms say "no more." You can add excitement and anticipation by adding a buildup such as "are you ready" or "get ready."

Baby Reads, Too

Hear the long series of syllables that Baby says as he looks at picture books? He's reading to you. Do read and discuss pictures with Baby often and allow him to join in. Baby understands much more than he can say. A love for and interest in books is an important step toward becoming a good reader.

Snap Caps

Gather an assortment of plastic bottles, small boxes, and their corresponding lids and tabs. With a piece of elastic and two plastic curtain rings, put the containers and lids together so that the rings are on the top side of the lid and bottom of the jar or box. String the elastic between the rings, through the inside of the container. Allow enough elastic so that when Baby pulls the ring the lid will snap to the container.

Direction Game

With Baby's receptive or understanding vocabulary he can now follow a few simple directions. This is very pleasing to everyone and can be great fun. You can begin to develop this new skill in simple games. For example, empty a basket or box of familiar toys onto the floor close to Baby. Now, while you hold the basket, ask Baby to bring you each item to refill the basket. Accept any object Baby brings. He is learning the concept of *bring me,* not that of identifying all the objects correctly. Just say, "Yes, you brought me a block," etc.

Poke Carton

Baby likes to explore holes and crevices with his probing forefinger. Use an egg carton to develop an easy game for Baby. To the inside lid of the carton, directly in line with each egg cup, glue some texture or object that would intrigue an exploring finger—fur, feathers, sandpaper, double-faced plastic tape. Securely tape the carton closed. With a sharp knife, cut a hole in the bottom of each egg cup through which Baby can stick his finger. Now allow Baby to discover this new game.

Outside

Playing outside is a delight for Baby. He will enjoy crawling and cruising about, but do keep an eye on him as he will try to eat grass, leaves, dirt, dead bugs, and anything else he may find. Although a little will not hurt him, it's a good idea to police the play area before Baby arrives.

Instant Toys

Band-Aid boxes are always fun toys—just the way they are with their easy to fasten tops and cozy storage space. Infants love to bang them, open them, shut them, and fill and empty them.

Recycling

Some of the earlier toys you have put away can now be recycled and used by Baby in a different way. He will enjoy having new toys every now and then, rather than too many all at once. Rattles can now be great drumsticks and teething beads something to dress up in.

Take-Aparts

Baby loves to take things apart, but, like most of us, he can't put together many of the things he took apart with ease. Take-apart games that are great fun include sorter boxes, puzzles, undressing dolls, and preschool toolbenches. Many of the safe but more sophisticated toys may be introduced now for their take-apart properties. Later they can be used for their other functions.

Painting

Now that Baby finger paints and uses a pastry brush, you might try several new ideas. Use adhesive tape to tape together three or four cotton swabs to use as a brush. Or, Baby might find an old toothbrush appealing.

Reassurance

Mothers of infants who paint with food report that their babies do not seem to play with their food more than do children who do not paint with food. Babies are smarter than that; they know the difference between mealtime and playtime. There does seem to be an earlier interest in self-feeding, however, on the part of babies who paint with food.

New Challenge

If Baby enjoyed playing with clothespins on a loaf pan last month, now is the time to add additional challenge to this game. Mix in a few spring-type pins for him to play with.

Winter Alternative

Flour or cornmeal play can be a winter alternative to water play. Place Baby in a wading pool on a discarded shower curtain or old sheet. Now give Baby a dishpan with about a cup or two of cornmeal or flour in the bottom. Add a few simple objects such as several cups, a funnel, plastic comb, etc. When Baby is finished, brush him off and shake the curtain or sheet outside. The birds will love you.

Paper Magic

Babies love paper. Keep a box of scraps for Baby. Include waxed, tissue, wrapping, cardboard, cellophane, brown, and flocked paper. On a day when nothing seems to interest Baby, this box might hit the spot.

Greeting Cards

Go ahead and save all those cards you receive and hate to throw away. Baby will appreciate them almost as much as you did. He likes cards for all occasions and will get lots of practice turning pages as he inspects them, especially if you seem interested, too.

Cards are also a great source for homemade storybook pictures. Cut out the rabbit, add a cotton tail, and you have the first page of a pat-and-touch book.

Doll Bath

Baby will enjoy giving his dolls a dunking in a dishpan. A few inches of water will be enough. Add a washcloth or sponge and maybe some bubbles. If you watch, you'll get a good imitation of Baby's interpretation of his own bath routine.

Game Chart

What games does Baby initiate?

_____

What games does Baby like best?

_____

What games does he play with siblings and friends?

_____

What games does he play with men?

_____

What games does he play alone?

_____

ROUTINE TIMES

BATHING

Steamy

If Baby's baths are steaming up the bathroom or kitchen, fill the tub or sink with a couple of inches of cold water before adding the hot water. This will keep windows and mirrors clean and clear.

The Duck

The classic bath toy and frequent companion of babies and young children is the rubber duck. Today ducks come in many colors, sizes, and materials. The very best duck floats and is not too tippy.

Here is a perky poem to share with Baby while he plays with his duck in the bath.

My-oh-my-oh-my what luck,
Here he comes, my rubber duck.
While I get my daily scrub,
Float him with me in the tub.
Stroke his back
And he will quack.
Rub a dub-dub.
Rub a dub-dub.

Faucet Fascination

Now that Baby is bathing in the tub, take this additional safety measure. Wrap the shiny faucet, a source of fascination, with a washcloth once the water has been drawn. Baby will be protected from touching a hot fixture and, should he wiggle, he will avoid a bump.

Tender Touch

Don't forget those little niceties. A squirt of baby powder or a splattering of lotion is an experience guaranteed to get a positive response. Sometimes we tend to skip these things as Baby grows older, but now is the time when Baby really appreciates them.

SLEEPING

PJs

Be very careful about sleepwear you choose for Baby. Sleeping bags and long nightgowns will get caught under his feet and may cause a baby who has begun to pull up to stumble and hit his head against the rail of the crib. Creepers or loose-fitting garments will allow greater freedom.

Night Owl

Baby may suddenly have become a night owl. The level of energy expended during the day may rouse him long after he has been put to bed. Parents who have just gotten used to a child's sleeping through the night may not appreciate this new routine. While there is little you can do to reverse this trend, do not promote this break in his schedule. Do not, for example, feed your wide-eyed baby. With small amounts of attention and a pat of affection, Baby will probably go back to sleep.

FEEDING

Don't Eat Too Fast!

By now Baby is undoubtedly fully involved with his own feeding. This messy process is not to be rushed. Baby may take anywhere from twenty to forty-five minutes to sample, fiddle with, and finally consume his meal.

Give Baby an opportunity to begin the meal by feeding himself. Later you may decide when it's time to help him finish.

Baby Utensils

Use plates and bowls with edges so that Baby has a surface against which to push his spoon. To keep plates or dishes from sliding away, attach small suction cups to their bottoms. For a change, present a meal in a TV tray, small baking pan, or colored paper plates or bowls.

A Drinking Problem?

Encourage neat drinking habits by pouring only a small amount of liquid into Baby's cup. Refill often.

Try a straw if Baby seems to be having trouble. Watch closely. He may not catch on.

We know of one mother who guided her baby's drinking by allowing her to use a sugar bowl. The baby held one handle, Mom the other.

Cleanup Tips

Baby usually finds feeding an absorbing and entertaining experience. It's all fine except for cleanup. Here are two ideas that should involve him and make the later part of the process relatively painless.
1. Oil him up! A thin, glistening layer of petroleum jelly or baby oil applied to cheeks and chin will protect skin and make cleanup quick.
2. Hand Baby a washcloth and let him spruce himself up. You may decide to finish the job, but Baby will appreciate a head start on the task.

Bibs

To cover, catch, and absorb is the aim of the bib. So, for a change of pace, tie on an old bandana or a lobster bib (share yours after the feast).

In an emergency, use safety pins and several layers of paper towel with a bottom layer of aluminum foil. Mold a drop catcher from a sheet of foil cut longer than the toweling.

Eating Song

To the tune of "Baby Bumble Bee":

I'm eating all the green peas I can see.
They're round and small and green as they can be.
So I'm eating all the green peas I can see.
Yummy, yummy, in my tummy,
Good for me!

Nonslip Seating

To keep Baby secure in his high chair while dining, add several nonskid appliqués or strips designed for the tub. We recently spotted some in the shapes of flowers, cartoon favorites, and geometric and free forms in bright colors.

DRESSING AND CHANGING

Ask for Help

Baby can begin to speed the routine of dressing if you give him adequate information. Remember that it is easier to pull down than push up. Start a T-shirt over his head and ask that he pull it down and push his arms through the holes. These directional terms are ones he will soon begin to appreciate.

Fancy Patch

The knees and bottoms of Baby's pants will soon start to show wear and tear. Patches on his corduroy coveralls can be a source of pleasure with a little imagination. Use prints, textures, or metallic-appearing mylar fabric for these reinforcements.

Shoe Biz

If Baby is crawling, he may require only socks or stockings. Soft slippers plus socks will keep toes warm if it's cold. Should Baby be a beginning cruiser, he may be pleased with soft booties or sneakers.

Perhaps Baby is walking and wearing his first shoes. To make those shoes work better, sand the soles to roughen them, or glue thin strips of foam rubber on them for traction.

The Terrific Star Chart

Your little achiever deserves the recognition that comes with recording, so get a pen or pencil and jot:

Baby's latest accomplishment:

_____

Dressing/undressing skills:

_____

Dining habits:

_____

Social skills/parlor tricks:

_____

HELPFUL HINTS

Develop Antennae

Don't be surprised to find Baby climbing upstairs, taking things apart on top of a table, etc. Silence is no longer golden (unless Baby is asleep); nowadays it's a state worth checking.

Baby, Books, and You

Baby deserves to have his own "working library." Develop one that will satisfy his fondness for variety and color by saving old magazines, catalogs, and worn-out children's books. Read a magazine together: an old one for Baby and a current one for you. After all, Baby wants to do as you do. Perhaps he prefers your lap over his own chair or the floor.

Reading out loud, no matter what the material, will please Baby; in fact, he will probably join in. This experience with books is the best sort of imitation and is educational as well.

An excellent way to limit Baby and save yourself from repeatedly reshelving your own collection of books is to pack them very tightly on the shelves. Those tricky fingers can be foiled.

Reminder

Baby is going through many impressive developmental changes. He is far from the predictable infant of a few months ago. Baby is capable of all manner of unexpected feats because of his mobility, agility, probing forefinger, and iron grasp.

The Talker

The best way to help Baby develop his language skills is for you to listen attentively. Response is important, too. Answering Baby in an appropriate adult manner will enhance his speech and language patterns.

Careful listening in the next few weeks may yield the "magic moment"—hearing Baby's first words. Even if this first word is not a real word, you will know it's what you've been waiting for because it will be used on an occasion when it clearly has specific meaning.

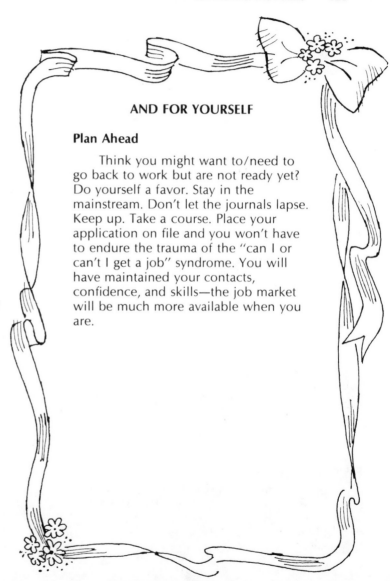

AND FOR YOURSELF

Plan Ahead

Think you might want to/need to go back to work but are not ready yet? Do yourself a favor. Stay in the mainstream. Don't let the journals lapse. Keep up. Take a course. Place your application on file and you won't have to endure the trauma of the "can I or can't I get a job" syndrome. You will have maintained your contacts, confidence, and skills—the job market will be much more available when you are.

Planter Priorities

Ah, plants—beautiful to behold, living things to nurture, accents to your decor, but a hazard to Baby. The moving, cruising ten-month-old may well be attracted to those robust plants. Some growing things are particularly poisonous. Others will give the taster a stomachache. Check with a reputable florist or greenhouse if you have questions.

Here is a partial list of plants you should keep out of Baby's way.

Azalea
Buttercup
Calla lily
Daffodil
Daphne
Diffenbachia
Elephant ear
Holly
Iris
Poinsettia
Oleander
Rhubarb
Wisteria

Don't let Baby drink water in which cuttings have been soaking, suck plants or stalks, or nibble leaves—these are toxic substances.

Unusual Appetite

Pica is a medical term given to a condition that occurs with some infants. These babies need special observation and protection because they crave inedible substances such as crayons, chalk, plaster, dirt, cigarettes, and paint chips.

A true case of pica is uncommon, but talk to your doctor if you feel that your child is unusually fond of eating nonfood substances.

Handiest Helper

The tool never to be without, especially now, is a large safety pin. Somehow having one or more available makes a busy parent or caregiver feel more secure. They are great for quick bibs, jacket closing, and other emergencies.

Patches

Keep patches on permanently by pinking the edges of iron-on tapes or patches. These are fun for Baby if cut in amusing shapes—free-form, geometric, animals, flowers, or favorite toys.

Netting

If you are an apartment dweller with a balcony or if you have a patio or deck that is aboveground, protect your baby by installing some sort of barrier. It takes a mobile infant little more than a split second to journey from the inside to the outside.

The fencing used around these outdoor places often has openings large enough for Baby to fit through. Check a hardware store for mesh nettings, chicken wire, or plastic screens that could be real lifesavers.

Strategy

Like most people, babies have trouble with impulse control. Moods rise and fall, tempers flare. Punishment is not very effective at this stage; in fact, it is a drain on adult energy. The best measure is prevention; plan ahead to avoid scenes.

Fingerprints!

Touching is a way of learning about the environment. Baby is not only touching everything, but he is also leaving his marks. Try some of these tricks to remove unwanted fingerprints.

—Chunks of stale bread can be rubbed over the marks
—A little dab of toothpaste on a damp cloth is a good way to remove fingerprints from the TV screen; rinse well
—A weak solution of baking soda and water makes a good spot remover

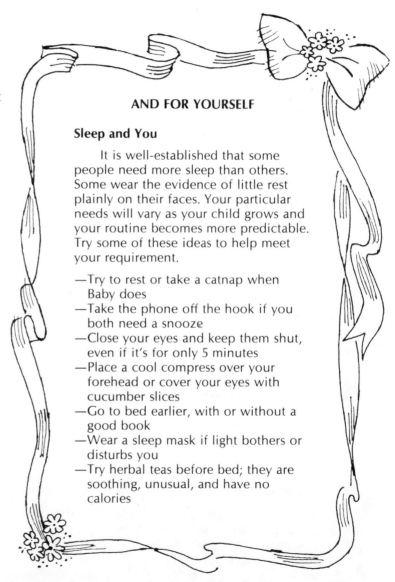

AND FOR YOURSELF

Sleep and You

It is well-established that some people need more sleep than others. Some wear the evidence of little rest plainly on their faces. Your particular needs will vary as your child grows and your routine becomes more predictable. Try some of these ideas to help meet your requirement.

—Try to rest or take a catnap when Baby does
—Take the phone off the hook if you both need a snooze
—Close your eyes and keep them shut, even if it's for only 5 minutes
—Place a cool compress over your forehead or cover your eyes with cucumber slices
—Go to bed earlier, with or without a good book
—Wear a sleep mask if light bothers or disturbs you
—Try herbal teas before bed; they are soothing, unusual, and have no calories

Orange Juice

To remove orange juice stains, presoak in cold water with enzyme-based detergents. This will lift the stains from the front of Baby's T-shirts.

Fido's Dish

The young activist has undoubtedly discovered your pet's dish. We know of one baby who surprised his parents by engaging in water play in liquid he found in the bowl. Splashing about and slapping the floor was a source of considerable pleasure and some mess. A great game idea, but a better idea is to plan ahead by selecting a container and setting the scene with an oilcloth.

And What About Fido?

Your pets are probably not as understanding as you are about having their mealtimes interrupted. To avoid mess and possible injury to Baby, plan to serve the pets in an inaccessible area.

By now your kitty litter should be out of Baby's reach.

PARENTS, FRIENDS, AND ADMIRERS

An Assist for Brothers and Sisters

Siblings may find dealing with a busy baby a trial. Older brothers and sisters may find that their possessions are suddenly no longer safe from a curious and cruising infant. Detouring Baby by taking items away seems to create a game situation. Baby thinks it's all a lark and is back for more, much to the frustration of his siblings. Your help in providing insight and strategies can promote understanding and harmony.

An Elephant for Lunch

As a special lunch treat or a snack, delight Baby and his siblings with a menagerie of animals. Use your imagination or an animal-shaped cookie cutter to shape the bread. If you use two slices of bread, the animals will stand by themselves. Spread toast with cream cheese or peanut butter. Fill sandwiches with any of Baby's favorites.

Dog and Cat Alert

Fido and Kitty will require more attention and affection from you in the coming weeks. Now that Baby can squeeze, poke, and pull with greater efficiency, your pets may find themselves in greater peril. Baby may decide that he can really chase this prey. Keep alert to safeguard both Baby and pet. It's not a good idea to leave these two alone.

We assume that the pet's shot record is up to date and complete just in case a nip occurs.

Grandpa's Light Show

This simple game involves light, shadows, and hands. In a darkened room, project a beam of light from a projector or a flashlight against a wall. Then make shadow animals with hands and props. This event recently staged by a grandpa thrilled Baby and siblings alike.

Grandma's Game

One granny delighted her grandchildren with this old finger play:

Here are Granny's spectacles
  (fingers form glasses placed up by eyes).
Here is my cap
  (bring fingertips together and place over head).
This is the way I fold my hands
  (fold hands)
And put them in my lap
  (place hands in lap).

Better Than a Kiss

With the many bumps, tumbles, and crashes Baby is taking these days, a collection of decorated Band-Aids makes a thoughtful gift. Make your own by keeping a package of self-adhesive dots next to your supply of Band-Aids. Add stars, stripes, or drawings with permanent magic markers. This surprise for Baby could be the beginning of a family tradition and a must for a toddler. Take a few with you when you travel by car or carriage.

Busy Baker

All of us are concerned about the amount of sugar children eat. For those who would love to bake for Baby, may we offer this compromise? Try your famous cupcake or cookie recipe in a two-bite size pan often used for making candies or dainty teacakes. These delicious miniatures can get past even the most finicky mom.

A Quickie

A nimble-fingered admirer can knit or crochet a mitten string for Baby in a matter of minutes. All but impossible to find, these cords are indispensible for keeping mittens and other small items together.

Approach Is Everything

For friends and admirers who have few opportunities to visit Baby, here are some time-tested techniques for approaching Baby.

—Eyes first! Catch Baby's eye and smile.
—Win a smile! Get him to smile at you. Make a few funny faces.
—Speak! Say something to him. Use Baby's name. Say, "Hi, Chris, how are you, what are you doing?"
—Encourage him to come to you. If Baby seems reluctant, slowly move toward him but *do not* touch him. Continue to talk and smile.
—Get down. Squat or kneel to get on Baby's level.
—Spend time. Speak for a few minutes while on Baby's level. Encourage him to move toward you.

—Share! If you have a surprise (book, toy, etc.), now is the time to present it to Baby. Don't give it away—yet. Don't pick up Baby. Take his hand and see if he will sit down with you and investigate the present you've brought.
—Remember that slow starts often lead to the warmest sorts of relationships. The best things develop over time.

Baby's Feelings Will Be Known

At ten months, Baby shows us his opinions! They are:

EMOTION	EXPRESSED
Delight	_____
Anger	_____
Frustration	_____
Self-satisfaction	_____

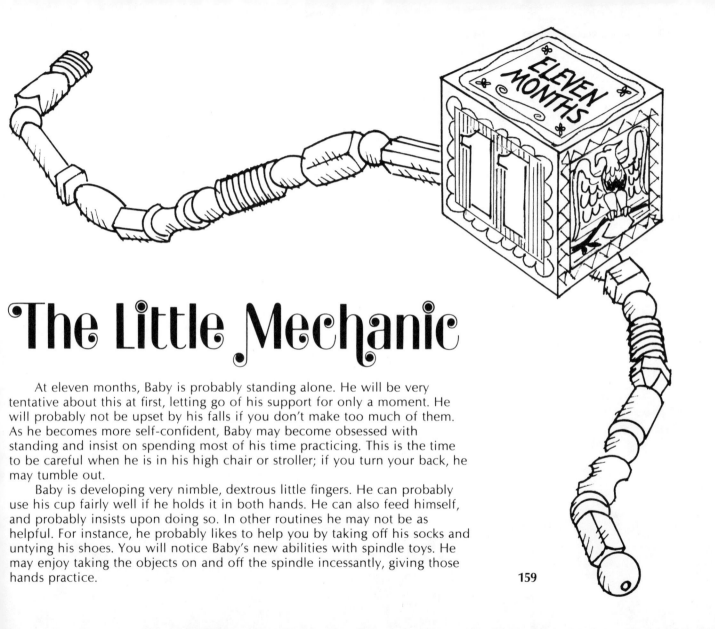

The Little Mechanic

At eleven months, Baby is probably standing alone. He will be very tentative about this at first, letting go of his support for only a moment. He will probably not be upset by his falls if you don't make too much of them. As he becomes more self-confident, Baby may become obsessed with standing and insist on spending most of his time practicing. This is the time to be careful when he is in his high chair or stroller; if you turn your back, he may tumble out.

Baby is developing very nimble, dextrous little fingers. He can probably use his cup fairly well if he holds it in both hands. He can also feed himself, and probably insists upon doing so. In other routines he may not be as helpful. For instance, he probably likes to help you by taking off his socks and untying his shoes. You will notice Baby's new abilities with spindle toys. He may enjoy taking the objects on and off the spindle incessantly, giving those hands practice.

159

Last month's imitation play is more marked now. Baby will follow you from room to room, assisting you in your chores. Encourage him to pick up or dust with you—he'll enjoy it and you'll get more done.

Baby's growing conceptual understanding of his environment can be observed in the way he relates to objects around him. Objects suddenly have definite, different properties. You may catch him swaying his toy airplane in the air, or racing his car along the rug.

Beginning with this month, Baby seems able to really differentiate between good and naughty behavior. He is starting to understand what pleases you and will consciously try to obey you and seek your approval. This may also be the month in which he begins real "testing" behavior; he is interested in knowing the limits you will impose.

ACTIVITIES, GAMES, AND SONGS

Dress-up

Baby is learning to do more for himself. He will enjoy a few dress-up items with which to practice. A diaper bag or purse, hats, and a few shoes, scarves, skirts, or shirts can be added to his play wardrobe. Of course, he may not wear the clothes appropriately, but he will admire himself in the mirror and entertain the entire family with his choice of adornment. Clothes that would fit an older child are the best size choice for this little performer.

Loving

Bring out the rejected stuffed animals. Now that one of Baby's latest tricks is to give affection, hugs, and kisses, he will enjoy showering his affection and tenderness on a multitude of play friends. It's rewarding to see Baby's awareness and imitation of the loving he's learned through your gentle care.

Chair Walker

You may find Baby is only interested in walking and that other activities frustrate him. Because he is a new or developing walker, his balance may not be up to his desire to go. Help Baby by giving him a fast-moving walker to push and hold as he scurries about. Any small wooden chair will do the trick. It can be tipped over so that the back is at an angle to the floor. This chair can then be pushed around the open play area by Baby as he relentlessly practices his walking skills. Felt adhesive dots will protect the chair and floor.

See What I Have

Baby comprehends many phrases such as "Show me what you have" and "Give it to Mommy." Baby is very proud of this new understanding and enjoys practicing these skills in a game. You can make up simple games. Give him simple directions and let him bring things to you.

Funny-Face Game

As you've noticed, Baby delights in mimicking other people's gestures. He can be caught scolding his bear just as you scold him.

You can turn this skill into a hilarious game by playing "Make My Silly Face." A mirror will help Baby get the nose wrinkle, wink, or frown just right. You may find him in front of the mirror some days later playing this funny-face game by himself or with a toy.

Puppet Friends

Remember the hand puppet you used in earlier months? Baby is now ready to try hand puppets on his own hands. You'll need to help him at first, but he will soon enjoy these new friends, especially in front of a mirror. This is also an entertaining game brothers and sisters can play with Baby.

A Ball for Baby

Let Baby play with a football this month. He will enjoy chasing this unpredictable rolling ball with its funny shape and texture.

Me Too

Baby will enjoy a game of flashlight play just like his older friends. A lightweight, disposable flashlight in a dimly lit room can be an excellent baby entertainer. Make sure that there are no removable parts to the flashlight; Baby's a good mechanic, given the opportunity.

Red Nose

Baby is beginning to be aware of the difference between himself and his mirror image. Play "Red Nose" with him to help develop this skill. Place a little blusher on a tissue and rub it on Baby's nose. Then let him see himself in the mirror. Does he notice his nose?

Flannelboard Fun

A flannelboard is a very versatile inexpensive toy; it is always welcome. Cover a piece of heavy cardboard with cotton flannel. For best results, use several layers of flannel or a layer of quilt-batting between the cardboard and the flannel. Lap-sized boards are nice as they can be easily transported and stored. Wallboards are also handy.

Simply cut out shapes of colored felt for Baby to arrange on the board. Pictures from magazines or old books can also be included if they are mounted on cardboard and felt is glued to the back of the cardboard. Baby will enjoy patting the picture and shapes onto the board and then peeling them off. Commercially produced items are available at school-supply stores; these include favorite storybook characters and learning sets.

Talk about and identify the objects on the board. Tell stories using the pieces. As you and Baby play with the flannelboard, his language skills will grow.

Teatime

Baby will enjoy a make-believe tea party with you and his stuffed friends. He will especially enjoy feeding them with his cup and spoon or sharing some cereal pieces or cheese squares.

Hinges, Latches, and Hooks

Baby will be intrigued with hinged boxes and cabinet doors. Latches and hooks can also be a source of problem solving. If you are handy with tools, make a busy board for Baby that includes these items. Or, have a friend make one.

Wooden or cardboard boxes, such as cigar boxes, will attract Baby's attention, especially if the box holds some of Baby's small toys.

A utility storage box like the ones used to store nails is also an excellent baby occupier. Its small drawers and many compartments are intriguing to explore. Later this box can be used for more complicated sorting and number games, or for storing childhood treasures.

Color Fun

A simple toy for a problem-solving baby is a clear plastic bottle, particularly one filled with colored water and securely sealed. Add a few pebbles for good measure. Baby will like shaking, turning, and studying this fascinating object.

Turn Toy

Baby loves to point to familiar pictures as you name them together. As a variation of the picture identification game, use a lazy Susan instead of a picture book. Simply cover the tray with paper and paste the pictures of familiar objects around the tray. Baby will enjoy helping you turn the lazy Susan and watching the pictures go around.

Self-Image

Baby's awareness of people is growing. He is noticing subtle details such as eyebrows, eyelashes, and freckles. If he has a baby doll with similar features, it will make comparisons easier. You may notice Baby at play closing the doll's eyelids and then his own eyelids.

Baby's Toys

This little action song will have special meaning for Baby now that he understands some of the words. The more you sing the song, the more fun it becomes.

Here's a ball for baby,
Big and soft and round
 (touch fingertips, forming ball).
Here's baby's hammer,
See how he can pound
 (pound one fist on other).
Here's baby's music,
Clapping, clapping so
 (clap hands).
Here are baby's soldiers,
Standing in a row
 (hold ten fingers erect).
Here is baby's trumpet,
Toot, too-too-too-too
 (pretend to blow trumpet).
Here's the way that baby
Plays at peek-a-boo
 (do peek-a-boo).
Here's a big umbrella,
To keep the baby dry
 (make an umbrella with hands).
Here is baby's cradle,
Rock-a-baby bye
 (pretend to rock a baby in your arms).

Winter Style

One mother decided not to store her child's inflatable beach toys. Instead, she weighted the inflated animals by partially filling them with water. They made lively playmates for her baby to push and poke; he would squeal with glee when they responded to his touch.

Home Movies

If you want an attentive audience for your home movies or slides, try Baby. You'll find he is delighted by the colorful images. He may even recognize his friends or himself. This can be a great game for all. So, don't save these treasures for a once or twice a year showing. Enjoy them often. They will help raise your spirits and remind you that these are the greatest times of your life.

Stories to Read

Baby loves being read to, especially stories that include animals and colorful illustrations. Consider these:

"The Three Little Kittens"
"The Three Bears"
"The Three Little Pigs"

At this stage, Baby is not able to follow a story plot; rather he is enjoying pointing and naming the pictures with you and, most of all, being close to you. Picture books that include clear colorful pictures of familiar objects are also a good choice.

Interlocking Blocks

Bristle blocks are an inexpensive, very versatile toy. These soft, safe interlocking blocks allow children to stick them together and form all sorts of wonderfully imaginative creations. They are also a good size to drop into all sorts of containers. Babies enjoy carrying these nubby pieces with them.

Hand Puppets

Baby will enjoy hand puppets made on the human hand. There are a variety; all are fun. Here are two easy ones.

1. Make a fist and place eyes on each side of the third knuckle of your index finger. With red paint or lipstick, color the inside of the index finger and thumb so that you have a mouth when you make a fist. If you move your fingers while in a fist, your puppet will look as if it were talking. Be as elaborate as you like; add a wig or a hat. Make a body and hold it in your fist to complete this little puppet person.
2. A second quickie involves making a hat for your thumb out of paper. Now draw a face on the area of the palm below the hat. As you move the thumb, Baby will enjoy watching the dancing, happy face.

ROUTINE TIMES

BATHING

Squeaky Clean

Here are some tips on shampooing Baby's hair.

—Remember to use baby shampoo; it is truly so mild that it doesn't sting when splashed into the eyes.
—Coat Baby's eyebrows and eyelids with a layer of petroleum jelly. This will cause soapy water to drip sideways instead of up and down. Having Baby watch in a mirror while you apply the petroleum jelly will help keep him calm.
—Slip a shower cap out of which the crown has been snipped onto Baby's head. This will reveal the back of Baby's head while protecting the front.

Soapy Sock

Baby will enjoy holding soap if it's in a nonslip sock (one of his). This is one way to let him hold soap and protect him from sampling it. Knot the top of the sock securely.

An Extra Tub

Should you find yourself visiting or traveling or just without a bathtub, try a small inflatable swimming pool. Simply position the pool in the shower stall and bathe baby as usual. Siblings will probably enjoy this novelty, too.

SLEEPING

Bedtime

Your live wire may find winding down an extremely frustrating part of his day. He will not give reliable signals as to when he is ready to rest. Stick with his scheduled bedtime and try this little poem as you make Baby comfortable.

Come little baby (or use Baby's name)
Calls the mother hen.
It's time to take your nap again.
And under her feathers
The little chick creeps.
And she clucks a song
Till he falls asleep.

Stars

Bring a little nighttime magic indoors. Cut several handfuls of stars out of luminous tape, or paint the constellations with a product guaranteed to glow in the dark. Arrange the twinkles on ceiling or walls of Baby's room. Don't forget the moon. Baby will be delighted when the lights go out.

A Few Golden Minutes . . .

If Baby is an early bird, try some of these measures to gain a few minutes of extra rest. Ignoring the jubilant shouts or initial cries of Baby is pointless. Instead make Baby comfortable.

—Change his diaper
—Offer him a drink
—Remove special sleep togs (sleeping bag, sacque, long nightie)
—Let in the light
—Move the crib toward a window; a birdfeeder or treats for feathered friends on a sill will make things more lively
—Supply a favorite toy or two
—Best of all, encourage an older brother or sister to come, stay, and play quietly. Baby can remain in his crib, which keeps both at a safe distance from each other

FEEDING

Worth the Wait

To manage mealtime preparation with a baby requiring distraction, occupy him with treats that will save his appetite.

—Discarded baseball cards
—Magazines, the glossier the better
—Old ribbons from gifts
—A bag with something grand to pull out, perhaps a long chain of knotted fabric strips or scarves

A Straw?

Just for fun, let Baby try a straw. Fruit juices or other healthy beverages are easy to follow in a nearly clear straw. Drink along with Baby to see if he can manage this trick.

Oh, Peanut Butter!

Parents concerned that their children are not getting enough protein should not overlook peanut butter. This very nutritious and comparatively inexpensive food is a real dietary standby. Many commercial brands are made with reduced salt and sugar. Or, make your own.

Combinations Baby will enjoy include:

—Peanut butter and lettuce leaf rollups
—Peanut butter balls with raisin centers rolled in carrot shavings
—Peanut butter with applesauce on toast strips (lady finger style)
—Pineapple tidbits frosted with peanut butter
—A peanut butter boat—long strips of banana filled with peanut butter

An Eating Buddy

If Baby is balking at mealtime, surprise him and invite a friend to join both of you. A doll wearing a bib or a puppet made of washable fabric holding a spoon may make the critical difference.

Carrots, Peas, and Spinach

Don't assume that Baby will not eat a food because he has refused it once. Babies are just beginning to develop preferences for tastes and textures. The best approach is to give him many opportunities to sample and experience foods he initially rejects.

When an item is pushed away, make a mental note to try it again several days later. Combining the new food with favorites is a good way to begin. Baby may relish combinations that are totally unappealing to everyone else. Remember that what Baby eats first has an effect on the taste of the next food. This awareness can work to the advantage of the feeder.

Calculated persistence and a willingness to be flexible seem to be the surest ways to get Baby to eat a well-balanced meal.

DRESSING AND CHANGING

A Dressing Helper

Plan ahead and set up a retrieving game rich in learning possibilities. Place Baby's pants and shirt in a low drawer or in a place he can reach so that he can bring them to you as dressing time approaches. This is an ideal time to help him with vocabulary and language skills.

Birthday Suit

Don't be surprised if you find a fast-fingered Baby who has taken off all his clothes, perhaps even his diaper. Resist an impulse to be angry, for this is actually an accomplishment. Dressing Baby in a one-piece jumpsuit or overalls will help keep this event from becoming a regular occurrence.

Tied!

Baby is definitely able to remove his shoes and socks. To prevent his doing so, try the good old double knot; it still works. Commercial gadgets are

fine, too; the bells and barrels that hold laces are helpful because they identify Baby's whereabouts while keeping shoes on and tied.

Changing

Some parents find that keeping a special toy or two—one for each hand—near the changing table takes the "wiggle out of the warrior."

Calamity

Baby is helping with his own dressing, mealtime is a mess, bedtime is all but impossible. Do record this month's routine calamities. Think for a minute and jot down the incident or two during which you might have cried except that they were *so* funny.

_____

_____

_____

_____

_____

_____

_____

_____

HELPFUL HINTS

Reminder

You really can't teach Baby how to walk. Baby will walk when he is ready. All that is necessary is that you provide him with a safe, interesting environment in which he can practice his emerging skills. Lots of tender loving care and encouragement will make a difference.

Exchange, Exchange

This is a fine stage or age to sort through Baby's clothing and gear. Prepare now for a swap with prospective parents or parents with toddlers. Baby clothes are rarely worn out because of infants' rapid growth. In a matter of months, clothes may be outgrown.

Don't overlook yard, garage, and thrift-shop sales. Spend money on good experiences and equipment for Baby rather than on clothes.

Fruit Soup

A change of pace for you and Baby is this recipe, delicious hot or cold.
1. In two cups fruit juice soak ½ to 1 cup dried, chopped fruit. (We like apple juice, apples, prunes, grapes, pears, oranges, apricots, and pineapple.) Allow to stand for 2 or more hours. Add honey to taste (1 Tbsp. to start).
2. Bring juice, fruit, and honey to a boil.
3. Mix 2 tsp. cornstarch with 1 tsp. water. Stir into mixture. Blend until mixture thickens.
4. Add 1 tsp. cinnamon.
5. To thicken and make more pudding-like, add more cornstarch. Float a bit of yogurt on top and dust with cinnamon.

An Extra Bed

Need an additional place to bed down a visiting infant, a sick baby, or a bored baby who needs a change of scene? Investigate these choices:

—a blow-up splash pool
—a playpen
—a rented port-a-crib

Another Drier

For families with the time, inclination, and preference for home cooking and food preservation, a fruit drier is a must. Baby and his family can enjoy fruit year round with this inexpensive piece of equipment, which can be found in organic food or hardware stores. When a favorite fruit—apple, peach, pear, apricot, or plum—is in season, an extra box or bag can be preserved without additives. The dried fruit will provide an excellent snack for dessert. It can be easily packed in a lunch bag or taken on trips.

Stroller Safety

Baby has become amazingly strong. More than one child we have known has reared up and pulled a stroller or buggy over on himself. Never, never leave Baby unattended in his carrier. Do not assume that he is safe while you are running an errand. Many strollers are unstable and have protruding parts or sharp edges. Check the weight limit on these portable wonders.

Neat Eatin' Ice Cream

How Baby adores the coldness and flavor of ice cream! If you can't persuade him to eat outdoors, cut a hole in a paper plate or small aluminum meat pan and poke the bottom of the cone through the hole. This is a fine time, too, for a quick mop-up with a premoistened cloth.

Circular Tip

Consider purchasing two plastic lazy Susans. With the growing supply of baby food in open jars, cans, and dishes, these disks will help keep your refrigerator organized. On the kitchen shelf, you can take a quick inventory with a slow spin of the Susan.

Just for Baby

A quick way to make a small table and chair for Baby is to cut down the legs of a piano bench, card table, or end table. Should you locate a small coffee table, no cutting will be necessary, as the table is already the right height. For small chairs, footstools or step-type stools are good alternatives. Preschool-size chairs are available commercially. Baby will enjoy his own furniture and will surprise everyone at how long he will sit in his own place.

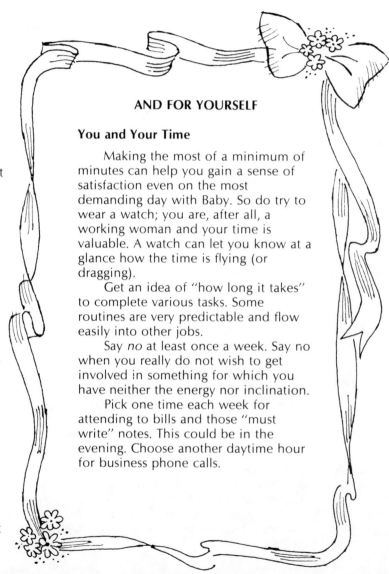

AND FOR YOURSELF

You and Your Time

Making the most of a minimum of minutes can help you gain a sense of satisfaction even on the most demanding day with Baby. So do try to wear a watch; you are, after all, a working woman and your time is valuable. A watch can let you know at a glance how the time is flying (or dragging).

Get an idea of "how long it takes" to complete various tasks. Some routines are very predictable and flow easily into other jobs.

Say *no* at least once a week. Say no when you really do not wish to get involved in something for which you have neither the energy nor inclination.

Pick one time each week for attending to bills and those "must write" notes. This could be in the evening. Choose another daytime hour for business phone calls.

Footloose

Baby receives much information about his world through his feet. These sensations can have an important effect on his learning to balance. Sometimes, it can be beneficial to delay the use of hard-soled shoes for a month or two as Baby experiments with pulling up, standing, or walking. Socks alone can be extremely slippery and dangerous; bare feet or slipper socks with nonslip soles are better choices.

Safety Hook

Bring a bit of peace to the household and install simple latch hooks, out of Baby's reach, of course. Brothers and sisters will especially appreciate this babyproofing technique because their possessions and territories will be protected. From the parent's or caregiver's point of view, this precaution minimizes worry when Baby is off exploring. This is an easy way to set limits.

Jars

Don't be overwhelmed or annoyed by the baby-food jars that may now be cluttering up your kitchen. Save them for a variety of uses throughout the home.

—In the workshop, nail lids onto a board or beneath a wooden shelf. The jars will clearly reveal nuts, bolts, washers, screws, and assorted nails.
—In the sewing room, the jars are ideal for snaps, hooks and eyes, buttons, bobbins, pins, thimbles, and needles.
—For gardeners, the jars are suitable for rooting cuttings or mixing small amounts of feeding solutions.
—For food preservers, the jars are a convenient way to create assortments of jams, jellies, or preserves for gifts.
—Freeze herbs and spices or potpourris in these small containers.
—Young artists will find the jars perfect for paint or water.

An Important Message

Should you plan to be away for the evening or several days, a cassette tape can maintain a link between you and Baby. Caregivers or baby-sitters will find these messages very helpful. Sing a favorite song or two and say good-night as you always do. This will make bedtime easier.

Still Sweet

Good old baking soda still sweetens. Try a solution of water and soda for plastic tablecloths, table mats, bibs, and other baby equipment that needs to be freshened up.

Irons

Hot irons always present a potential safety hazard. Place your hot iron on a back stove burner and make sure the cord is not in Baby's reach when you are cooling your iron.

PARENTS, FRIENDS, AND ADMIRERS

Brother and Sister

To help build a positive relationship between Baby and his siblings, help them discover games they can enjoy playing together. Suggestions include:

—Water play with measuring cups, spoons, funnels, and sponges
—Finger painting with colored dessert whip, pudding, or mashed potato flakes
—Playing "Roll the Ball"

You can also help older children accept Baby and his antics by letting them talk to you about their feelings. A good way to start such a discussion is to read a story about other children and their baby brothers and sisters. We suggest:

Couldn't We Have a Turtle Instead?
   by Judith Vigna
It's Not Fair by Robyn Supraner
I Don't Like Timmy by Joan Hanson
Tommy's Big Problem by Lillie D. Chaffin

Photo Flair

A great gift for Baby's first birthday next month is a personalized baby book from an admirer with photographic flair. A book of pictures of Baby's world would include Baby, his family, his pet, and his special friends. Don't forget his possessions: favorite toys, his cup, his crib, and maybe even his house. Such a book will be a favorite toy and a priceless keepsake, so make this chronicle of Baby durable—a real gift of love.

Baby Hand-Print Cookies

Make up your favorite sugar cookies or use ours, and use the imprint of Baby's hand as a cookie cutter pattern. Simply trace around Baby's hand on cardboard and cut out the pattern. (Baby will let you do only one or two directly from his hand.)

Sugar Cookies

⅔ cup shortening
¾ cup sugar
½ tsp. grated orange peel
½ tsp. vanilla
1 egg
4 tsp. milk
2 cups all-purpose flour
1½ tsp. baking powder
¼ tsp. salt

1. Cream together first four ingredients.
2. Add egg and beat until light and fluffy.
3. Stir in milk. Add remaining ingredients.
4. Divide dough in half. Chill one hour.
5. On a lightly floured surface, roll dough to ⅛-in. thickness. Cut out hands with a knife. Bake on greased cookie sheet at 375° F for about 6 to 8 minutes. Cool slightly and remove from sheet to cool. Makes about 2 dozen cookies.
6. Decorate with frosting, nails, or rings, as desired.

Baby and his family will enjoy these good-tasting cookies. This pattern can be used with bread dough, too. You might want to save a bread dough sample to shellac and make into a kitchen plaque for an admirer.

Birthday Present

Start now if you are planning to make or build a gift for Baby's very first birthday. Remember to make clothing somewhat larger than his current size—he's still growing fast.

Special Day

Brothers and sisters deserve a day with you and without Baby. Do plan a very special time together when you can be all theirs. How about a trip to the ice cream parlor, the zoo, or a fast-food restaurant after the park? It will make them much more willing to have Baby come along most of the time if they know they can look forward to these regular, special times.

Bronzing Baby's Shoes

Want to preserve Baby's first shoes without spending a lot of money? Fill them with plaster of Paris and spray with gold, silver, or bronze paint. You'll be delighted with their professional look.

Help the Baby-Sitter

Even the best baby-sitter will do a better job if he or she has more knowledge about his or her charges. You might want to show to your sitter the following list, or copy and post it for him or her. Do add your own ideas. Update often as Baby grows.

Best snack _____

Where _____ How Many _____

Favorite music _____

Location _____

How Baby likes to be comforted _____

_____

Bedtime ritual _____

_____

Favorite toy _____

Books to read and talk about _____

_____

_____

Location _____

Baby-sitters need ideas about how best to help Baby enjoy himself while you are away. Besides giving information on Baby's routines, tell them about Baby's favorite games and songs. Keep a few of these on index cards to share with the baby-sitter; this can make the evening more fun for everyone. Encourage baby-sitters to think of some of the favorite songs they remember from their early years and to jot them down. You and Baby will enjoy learning some new ones, too. Baby will soon begin to associate the baby-sitter's arrival with song-and-game times, making your departure much easier.

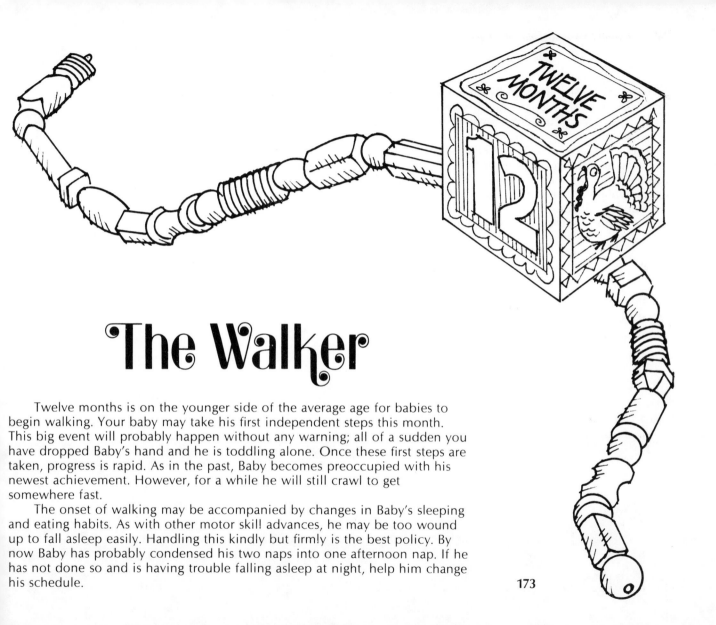

The Walker

Twelve months is on the younger side of the average age for babies to begin walking. Your baby may take his first independent steps this month. This big event will probably happen without any warning; all of a sudden you have dropped Baby's hand and he is toddling alone. Once these first steps are taken, progress is rapid. As in the past, Baby becomes preoccupied with his newest achievement. However, for a while he will still crawl to get somewhere fast.

The onset of walking may be accompanied by changes in Baby's sleeping and eating habits. As with other motor skill advances, he may be too wound up to fall asleep easily. Handling this kindly but firmly is the best policy. By now Baby has probably condensed his two naps into one afternoon nap. If he has not done so and is having trouble falling asleep at night, help him change his schedule.

173

Baby's newest sounds and words relate to his expanding understanding of object classification. He may identify animals or vehicles by making the sounds they make. Don't let Baby fool you; he understands many of the things you are saying to him.

The awareness of his own behavior, which began about a month ago, is increasing as toddlerhood approaches. He is testing limits constantly. He may even begin having real tantrums. The best way to handle this is to define rules that allow Baby freedom to grow but do not impinge on other members of your household. These rules must be consistently enforced. Heading off trouble before it starts is the best way to begin Baby's second year.

ACTIVITIES, GAMES, AND SONGS

A Ball for Baby

Baby will love an airy lightweight plastic ball, the kind with all the holes. These balls are great for little pitchers to practice throwing; they are also easy to hold and retrieve.

Race Car Driver

Baby will enjoy wheeled toys he can push and watch roll. Make a cardboard hill and track from a discarded paper box. Show Baby how to start his cars down the hill. He will enjoy retrieving his cars and repeating this game. Baby's enjoyment and excitement will be enhanced by your encouragement and help.

Hairdresser

Baby will like playing with his own comb and brush in front of the mirror. He will also make a game of brushing and combing his doll's and stuffed animal's hair. You can turn this into a learning time by talking to him and encouraging his efforts.

Wiggles

This little poem will be a favorite for years. Baby will soon learn to go through the motions himself with your help. Just do as the words suggest. A home movie of this would be a treasure, capturing Baby's fleeting days of babyhood. Next month he becomes a toddler.

I wiggle my fingers.
I wiggle my toes.
I wiggle my shoulders.
I wiggle my nose.
Now the wiggles are out of me.
See how still I can be.

Roller Fun

Your old plastic hair rollers make great toys. These graduated cylinders can be strung as beads or used to fill a busy baby's many containers. If you happen to have a deluxe set with its own holder for easy storage, it is truly a find. Baby will spend hours arranging the rollers on the holder pegs.

The rollers are easy to wash and almost indestructable. Remember, you slept on them for years.

Matching

Matching simple objects and pictures is lots of fun and a learning game, too. Cut out pictures of several objects that look like Baby's toys. Mount them on cardboard and cover with clear contact paper for durability.

Lay three or four of the pictures on the floor in front of you and Baby. Name the pictures and point to them as you and Baby identify them. Now hand Baby the object that matches the picture. Show him how to place the shoe on the picture of the shoe. Now, with the same object, let Baby do it by himself.

Lavish Baby with praise for his efforts. Good starting objects include shoe, cup, baby doll, and a favorite stuffed animal. The important thing is that the items be very familiar to Baby, things he knows and likes to talk about.

Something Different

A new twist for an old toy is to hang Baby's giant inflatable beach ball from the ceiling so that Baby can walk under it and push it out of the way. He will enjoy this new responsive toy that bounces back when pushed aside. Soon he will be scurrying under it with glee.

First Rider

Baby's first riding toy is a landmark purchase, exciting for all. Choose one without pedals, as the skill of pedaling does not come for some time. Baby will literally wear the wheels off this toy in the months ahead.

See this month's "Helpful Hints" for several suggestions on how to apply a furniture-saving bumper to the front of this favorite toy. You'll want to designate an open, safe area where riding is allowed, one where Baby can ride with abandonment without damaging himself or the house.

Street Strut

Baby wants to walk! You may find that the best way to keep the enjoyment in your outings is to let Baby help you push his stroller on your walks. This will give him extra stability, balance, and confidence. Your very independent baby may even be a willing rider on the return trip.

Conversion

Remember the cardboard sit box described in Chapter 3? This box can easily be converted into a new toy—or use any cardboard box of about 9 in. x 12 in. x 9 in. Attach a body or shoulder strap and cut out the bottom of the box. This gives Baby something to wear. Add a head and tail and Baby can be a unicorn, cow, or lion. Add paper-plate wheels and paper-cup headlights and you have a car. This is special fun when Baby can watch himself in a mirror.

Carpet Puzzles

Carefully cut several shapes from a square piece of carpet about 12 in. x 14 in. in size. From several other scraps of carpet, contrasting in texture and color to the first, cut the same shapes. These shapes will be the pieces in the "form board" you cut first. The form board can be glued to a piece of plywood. Baby will enjoy this colorful puzzle with its fuzzy shapes. Although he cannot yet master this puzzle by himself, he can enjoy using its parts in many ways of his own devising. As a toddler, he will learn to master the puzzle.

Color Wise

Providing Baby with early opportunities to experiment with colors is a very beneficial learning process and fun for Baby. Paint three coffee cans, boxes, or baskets the three primary colors—red, blue, and yellow. Now gather objects such as wooden blocks, rubber balls, etc., of each color to be placed in the correctly colored container. Only a few objects are necessary for each container. Play the game of sorting together. With practice and experience, Baby will learn to play this game alone. He will be extremely proud of this skill once mastered.

Rocking

Many babies gain endless pleasure from a small child's rocker, especially if someone else in the family also uses a rocker. These rockers are relatively inexpensive and can often be found at neighborhood garage sales. Rocking provides Baby with an outlet; he can keep moving while he stays nearby.

Card Deck

Busy babies enjoy rustling through things. A picture card deck can provide this opportunity. Simply cut into quarters the fronts and backs of several old manila folders. Place a bold picture of one of Baby's things on each card. Now cover with clear contact paper.

If possible, make pairs of pictures. Baby will enjoy trying to match these pictures; he has a 50 percent chance of guessing the right answer.

There are many fun games you can play together with his cards.

—Turning them all over
—Turning them all right-side up
—Saying them and giving them to each other one by one
—Dividing them in half and each laying one down

These very simple games promote complex learning later.

Presto Puppets

You don't have to be creative to make a sock puppet. They are so easy you will wonder why you never thought of them yourself. Just put a sock on your hand; the heel should be on top of your wrist. Stuff the toe back towards your palm, between your fingers and thumb. This makes the mouth. Now take the sock off and sew the corners where you pinned to hold the mouth in place. Add button eyes and nose, hair, ears, etc. Easy, quick, and fun, this is a great family project for a rainy afternoon.

No Cleanup

Baby loves to paint. For those days when you just don't have the time to get everything together, Baby will be just as happy to paint with a little colored water on the sidewalk, the fence, trees, etc. Exterior painting can be just as much fun and there is almost no cleanup. The only supplies you need are brush, bucket, water, and Baby. Several sizes of brushes add to the excitement.

Baby's Play

As this year draws to a close, reflect on Baby's play. Jot down the year-end favorites.

Song/finger play _____

Game _____

Story _____

Trip _____

Bowling

Soda pop cans make great bowling pins for Baby. Add a few pebbles for weight and then tape them shut. To add a shape, stuff the toe of an old sock and pull it down over a can and secure at the bottom. Now use a ribbon or rubber band to form the proper small bowling pin shape at the top of the sock. Add funny faces if you like. Baby will enjoy scattering these pins with his rubber ball and then setting them up again.

Books

Although Baby is still not quite ready to follow a story and your reading is really picture naming, it's not too early for nursery rhymes. These melodious tales with their funny words are fun to listen to even if their meaning is unclear. Some of the best are the sing-song type such as "Three Little Kittens."

Invest in a good book of Mother Goose rhymes. Your local children's librarian will have many suggestions of ones to buy. She or he can also suggest storybooks for admirers who want to start Baby's library. Take Baby on his first trip to the library. Start his second year off in a learning way.

Blanket Fun

Baby will love a ride on a blanket being pulled along the tile or wood floor. He will be excited by this new way of traveling. Because he is close to the ground, it is safe if done with slow stops and starts. One mom found this great fun for laundry times. As she stripped the beds, she gave Baby a ride from room to room.

Cleanup

Yes, someone in your house will enjoy cleaning with you. Give Baby a sponge or dustcloth and let him clean as you do, perhaps a low table or other accessible surface.

One mother made a glove duster for her baby. She sewed yarn pom-poms onto the palm side of a child's mitten. All her child had to do was wipe over the dusty surface. He thoroughly enjoyed the mitt with its funny features and spent many happy moments cleaning.

Sorting Boxes

Sorting boxes with a variety of different-shaped holes can now be used by Baby if you give him the right object to push through the hole.

For variety, cut different shapes and sizes out of foam rubber and cover them with colorful fabric. Baby can stuff them in any hole with great success. Save the wooden or plastic shapes that come with the box for later.

ROUTINE TIMES

BATHING

Slip Stoppers

It seems that slips and mishaps occur most frequently when putting Baby into or taking him out of his bath. Now that he may try to get out himself, consider arranging nonslip bath strips in a pattern on the inside of the tub and along the top ledge. This measure will minimize the hazard of entry and exit.

Shampoo

Many babies hate to have their hair washed because the water runs into their eyes. To stop this, fold a washcloth lengthwise and lay it on Baby's forehead. Ask him to follow some simple directions while you rinse his head. It's a game. Have Baby look up and tell you what he sees, look down, and so on. Letting Baby participate in bathtime makes it easier and more pleasant for everyone.

Peek-a-Boo Face Wash

Stop fighting with Baby at face-washing time; play a game of peek-a-boo instead. Lay the washcloth on Baby's face, rub it around, and lift it off with a peek-a-boo. Try it, it really works.

Octopus

A bath toy that pleases Baby this month is an octopus made of a whiffle or styrofoam ball, cotton cord, and a rubber band. Drape the cords over the ball and attach with the band. For added fun, draw on a face with an indelible marker or sew on buttons for eyes.

Old Bathtime Goodie

Rub-a-dub-dub
Three men in a tub,
And who do you think they be?
The butcher, the baker, the candlestick maker.
Turn 'em out, knaves all three.

SLEEPING

Zzzzzzz

On Baby's party day, try to stick to his routine as closely as possible. Make sure that Baby has napped before the festivities begin. If you are especially lucky, he will nap for an extra few minutes, which will allow the star of the party to be in fine shape. Remember: parties are not a production, they're fun.

Sleepy Time Rhyme

Wee Willie Winkie runs through the town,
Upstairs and downstairs in his nightgown,
Rapping at the window, crying through the lock,
"Are the children all in bed, for it's eight o'clock."

Two or More

Most babies take pleasure in having familiar toys or cuddly objects with them when they are put down for a nap or to bed for the night. These items become increasingly significant to a child who associates them with comfort. He knows them completely through his sense of touch and his sense of smell. Avoid a distressing situation by identifying these objects and buying or setting aside duplicates now. These favorites will inevitably grow worn, soiled, and disreputable looking. Make no mistake, however; Baby will most likely search for these objects and may not sleep without them. If you replace his cherished object with a duplicate, he will know instantly that this is not his old cherished object. He may, however, be willing to accept a look-alike substitute should the original become lost.

FEEDING

Tasty Bag

As you prepare a meal for a cranky baby who is unwilling to wait, or if you find that there will be an unavoidable delay, placate him with a "tasty bag"! Place several tidbits in a brown paper bag for Baby to find, feel, and sample.

Joining In

Baby may have indicated that more than anything he would like to eat with the rest of the family. One way to let him be part of the scene is by providing him with a matching place mat cut to fit his tray.

If Baby refuses to eat alone, remove his tray and allow him to use the table surface while strapped into his chair. Baby wants to be part of this typically social time.

Dining Tip

For special occasions, or eating-out situations, remember that, of all the people in the party, Baby is the youngest and the least able to wait. It is wise to carry a few snacks with you so that Baby will manage the waiting period with less displeasure.

Fancy Food

Add a little zest and touch of elegance to mealtime. Force mashed potatoes or carrots through a pastry tube and swirl into a small peak on Baby's plate. He'll enjoy the fancy fare.

A Change in Position

Losing patience with a finicky eater? A little change can make a great deal of difference. Let Baby sit next to a sibling or special admirer. You may both enjoy the experience and eat more of the meal.

DRESSING AND CHANGING

Shoes/Sneakers?

There is a lot of controversy about when Baby should have his first shoes. There are questions and opinions about the type and quality of the shoes; soft or hardsoled; high, low, or knit tops. The few points that experts seem to agree upon are:
1. Importance of a good fit—take him with you.
2. Shoes should never be so big that Baby may trip.
3. Sole should have a tread or some nonslip finish.
4. Shoes should be flexible.
5. Interior of shoes should be checked to ensure that there are no rough seams that could cause blisters or other discomfort.

Baby's First Shoes

Date purchased _____

Size _____

Style _____

Color _____

Store where purchased _____

Baby's reaction _____

_____

Socks Up

Tired of hassling with Baby's socks—no matter how you try, the pairs never match. Try this little trick. On the heel of each pair of socks you buy, place a symbol with a laundry marker. It takes the snarl out of matching Baby's socks. When Baby is older, he can learn to do this matching trick himself.

Reach In

We have noticed that many babies intensely dislike getting into their jackets or coats. One reason could be that small fingers are frequently bent while arms are thrust into a garment's sleeves. This jamming can be avoided if you reach into the sleeve to meet a small hand halfway.

Roll 'em Up

When it comes to fashion, Baby would thoroughly appreciate it if those who dress him would always remember to roll up his pants legs until they just graze his ankle. "Short" is a safe and comfortable length for a walking baby. Because of his ample, round belly, the most comfortable waist size will usually be accompanied by pants with legs that are *much* too long, so roll 'em up, please.

A Penny Spent . . .

Do you find it difficult to settle on a disposable diaper that fits an increasingly active and growing child? Fit is critical; it is a significant consideration when attempting to avoid accidental damage to furniture and rugs. A bit of time and a few pennies more may well help minimize aggravation. All disposables are not the same; all disposables do not have the same absorbency and fit. Ask other parents for their recommendations.

HELPFUL HINTS

Reminder

Baby's first steps are far more important to adults than to the child himself. Each baby is very different and has his own unique set of priorities. So do not be overly concerned if Baby is so pleased with his agility in crawling that he shows little more than a passing interest in walking. He will, soon!

For Safety's Sake

Even with special latches and rearranged shelves, Baby and siblings may still get too close to dangerous cleaning agents. Set up your own code system to keep everyone just a little bit safer.

Hang a small bell around the top of all toxic bottles, cleaners, and medicines. To remind yourself which bottles contain poisons, put bright orange mystic tape or permanent magic marker stripes around those that hold poisons.

Tape down the tops or completely seal lids of special cleaners after each use.

NEVER rely completely on the child-proof lid.

Helpfuls from You

What has helped the most this year? Take a minute or two, which may be all you can spare, to jot down some things too good to forget.

Supportive services, agencies, and groups:

Agency   Service   Address   Phone

_____

_____

Best books or magazines (some clarified issues, others raised questions):

_____

_____

_____

Keep as references:

_____

_____

Greatest time (energy) savers:

_____

_____

Splinters Out

Should your adventurer reveal a wooden splinter or two in his finger, use this fairly painless way to remove it. Soak the finger in vegetable oil and then numb it with an ice cube. Now you can remove the splinter.

Or Gum

A sibling may share his or her gum or Baby may happen upon it himself. In either case, gum is easily removed from hair with cold cream or peanut butter. Next it's into the tub for a bath and shampoo. Ice will help remove gum from clothing. Rub over the area and scrape off the hardened portion. Or soften gum with an egg white, scrape, then launder as usual.

Trash

Just as pets are tempted by aromas and must check them out, so is Baby. He will certainly investigate the trash bins, garbage pails, and wastepaper baskets. He may well try to pull the container over, just to see if there is anything good inside. He will enjoy dumping the low cans for the sheer pleasure of watching items roll or fall out. He may also try to sit in any of these cans. Prepare for these possibilities by:

—Placing a large brick or other weighty object between the garbage can and the liner, so the container will be less easily upset
—Separating out disposable items that may be harmful to Baby. Place them in a container that always remains within a latched cabinet
—Giving Baby his own trash in his own sack or basket

Advice Column

A friend is planning and preparing for a new baby. Now that you are an "experienced hand" what specific information or advice would you share?

Games and activities _____

_____

_____

Routines _____

_____

_____

Self-care _____

_____

_____

Dealing with others _____

_____

_____

Toys

Now may be the time to give Baby's toys a scrub down. Squeak toys will survive the wash if the outlet is completely taped.

Many rubber toys will tolerate the gentle agitation of a washing machine, especially if placed in a net bag.

Not What It Seems

It's not like they said it would be. What myths could you dispel regarding a year's worth of life with a baby?

_____

_____

_____

Quick Cleanup

A hint (from Chapter 10, "Routine Times") that will minimize fuss on the Big Day (Baby's first birthday) is to "oil him up." Lipstick, frosting, and other sweet treats can be easily removed from Baby's face if this procedure is followed before you sit down to celebrate.

Grape Juice

Only chlorine bleach will remove grape juice from Baby's clothing.

Camera

This is a party month so plan ahead. Get your camera ready to record the events. Check to see that the batteries are working, that a supply of film, flashbulbs, and other necessary lighting fixtures are within easy reach. Don't miss a single exciting pose.

Stains and Spots

If stains and spots are a problem (and spray-on pretreating solutions and washing aids are too expensive to use) consider using some of your spray-on all-purpose household cleaners. These are much cheaper and many mothers report they work even better.

Cushion the Crash

Now that Baby is using his riding toys and pushing his trucks and cars about, try this measure. Cut foam rubber bumpers to fit Baby's vehicles. These bumpers can be covered with durable fabric and attached directly to the toys with special glue. Not only will these additions add pizzazz to Baby's toys, they will also prevent nicks and scuffs to the furniture, walls, and woodwork. The bumpers can be purely utilitarian or as artistic and imaginative as you wish.

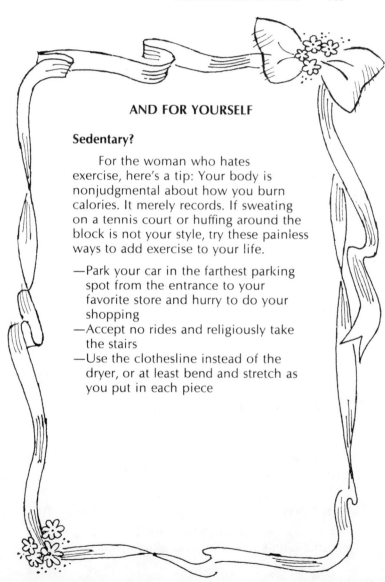

AND FOR YOURSELF

Sedentary?

For the woman who hates exercise, here's a tip: Your body is nonjudgmental about how you burn calories. It merely records. If sweating on a tennis court or huffing around the block is not your style, try these painless ways to add exercise to your life.

—Park your car in the farthest parking spot from the entrance to your favorite store and hurry to do your shopping
—Accept no rides and religiously take the stairs
—Use the clothesline instead of the dryer, or at least bend and stretch as you put in each piece

Sitter

Some parents have found that hiring a baby-sitter for Baby's first birthday is a lifesaver. If Baby should demand more than he usually does, due to the arrival of guests or excitement, there will be a familiar set of hands to take extra special care of his needs. Once his presents have been opened and his time in the limelight has ended, the sitter can entertain him in his room, leaving his parents free to entertain adult guests without worry. This added flexibility will allow you to celebrate, too—after all, what an accomplishment!

Storage

If Baby's room is becoming overrun with bulky stuffed toys and animals, reclaim the floor by thinking "up." Hang a lightweight wooden ladder horizontally about 2 feet from the ceiling. This aerial shelf will keep favorite toys clean and within view, and will add interest to Baby's quarters.

Or, hang a short ladder vertically for an instant set of shelves.

Corner Interest

With a continually growing toy collection and with bulky items scattering themselves about the house, we like this "cleanup corner" strategy! One friend utilized a corner space by stringing fabric from one cup hook to another. Toys were instantly concealed behind the curtain. As her child grew, she fashioned the front of a house out of oilcloth, complete with windows, doors, and roof. By day the "house" was a versatile, dramatic play center; at cleanup time it became a warehouse behind which favorites rested close by but out of sight. She bumper-proofed the walls and moldings so that toys could even be ridden into the corner.

PARENTS, FRIENDS, AND ADMIRERS

Grandmothers Only

Only Grandma would remember such a special gift on Baby's first birthday, the "Birthday Bib." Do waterproof this family treasure to preserve it for the babies to come.

Party Goers

Even if you are a habitual early bird, do try to give the birthday family an extra ten minutes before you arrive for the party, and don't plan to stay too late. This thoughtful gesture will be most appreciated by your friends.

A Special Friend

Help siblings feel that they are a part of the excitement on Baby's party day by allowing them to invite a special friend over to play. This will assure that they will enjoy themselves, too.

Across the Miles

A nice way to share the fun and excitement of Baby's first birthday party with grandparents who cannot attend is to tape the event. The tape can be sent with the pictures to add the enjoyment of sound.

Good Gift

Baby will like a small preschool slide. He will quickly learn to enjoy this new sensation with your help and insist on many turns. Preschool slides are very common and can often be found at local garage sales at bargain prices.

Photo Uses

Now is the time for photos. Do take a good one of Baby and his cake. Have an 8 x 10 print made for a puzzle. Cut a piece of Masonite, the size of the picture, into puzzle pieces. Now, with a mat knife, cut the picture into the same-shaped pieces. Glue the picture to the pieces of wood. Shellac each piece. You will have a personalized puzzle that will provide hours of fun.

A Friend's Gift

Give close friends a special treat for Baby's birthday. Call ahead so that a baby-sitter can be arranged for and ask your friends if you can treat them to dinner and a quiet drink following the party. Help them unwind and relax. There's something so nice about walking away and worrying about cleanup tomorrow.

Gift Ideas

Here are some gift suggestions for the year-old baby.

—A T-shirt with a big number one
—An outdoor swing with supports
—A small xylophone with attached stick for Baby to bang on
—Colorful pull toys that make noise
—Small riding toys without pedals
—A large, colorful ball

Speaking of Gifts . . .

To help reduce sibling anxiety, a special friend might bring brother or sister a small gift, too. Baby won't know the difference, but the older child surely will!

My Gift

Siblings will want to make or buy a very special gift for Baby, too. Help them do so. It is important that they have confidence in their gift. Here are some suggestions.

—A family picture book that includes favorite photos and pictures they've selected, drawn or cut out, and mounted.
—An enterprising young artist (eight years or older) may want to attempt a real painting of Baby. Poster paint can be used on an inexpensive canvas or have them use water colors on paper.
—A batch of homemade peanut butter play dough with several plastic cookie cutters. The dough will last for several weeks if kept in the refrigerator.

EDIBLE PLAY DOUGH

1 jar of peanut butter (18 oz.)
6 tbsp. honey (or to taste)
Add nonfat dry milk and knead to the right consistency.

Family Gift

Want to give a gift for the whole family? How about matching family sweatshirts or T-shirts? The Three Bears—Momma, Papa, and Baby—is one possible theme.

Thank You

If you hate to write thank-you notes, consider using one of the photos taken at Baby's party for a photo thank-you card just like the ones used at Christmas. Baby's admirers will be pleased.

An Alternative

In lieu of a large party for Baby's birthday, you may want to start a tradition of taking a special trip as part of the birthday celebration. Choose a trip to the zoo or another special place that will be a treat every year for years to come.

Reflections

You've made it through the first year. Baby isn't the only one who's grown and changed; you have, too. Take this time to reflect on your first year with Baby—a pause before toddlerhood.

_____

_____

_____

_____

_____

_____

_____

_____

_____

Baby's Gift to Someone Else

Would you believe that babies enjoy gluing? Tape a piece of paper on Baby's high-chair tray. Sprinkle a little glue (white) on the page. Give Baby some colorful scraps of paper or fabric. Show him what to do and let the artist work. When the artist seems satisfied, retrieve the creation and mail to proud grandparents, relatives, or friends. This might make a nice card for Mom and Dad, if done at a caregiver's.

APPENDIX A

HANDLING THE FUSSY BABY

Babies cry because it is their only way to summon help to meet their needs. You do not need to worry about spoiling a young infant. In fact, research suggests that the best way to decrease Baby's crying is your consistent responsiveness to his cries.

There are degrees of crying. Imagine Baby's cries as running along a continuum; he starts with a fussy, halfhearted cry that eventually develops into a panicky, desperate cry of rage. Your response is most effective if it comes before this final, desperate stage.

As Baby becomes secure in your ability to meet his needs, his crying diminishes and becomes more of a select signal. As you learn Baby's ways, you will be able to distinguish between a cry of hunger and one of pain. As Baby grows and develops, his routines will become more regular. Since you will be increasingly able to anticipate his needs, you can cut down on his crying by eliminating problems before they happen.

The first thing to do when Baby cries is to run through a checklist of possible problems. We suggest the following:
1. Is Baby hungry or thirsty?
2. Does Baby have a gas pain or a need to burp?
3. Does Baby need a diaper change or some fresh ointment on his bottom?
4. Is Baby tired?
5. Is Baby too hot or cold? (Use the temperature of his back or tummy as an indicator.)
6. Is Baby lonely or is there too much stimulation?
7. Does Baby need to suck?
8. Is Baby sick? Is he running a temperature? Are there any other symptoms?

Babies cry for a reason. Unfortunately, we are not always able to determine just what the reason is. If you can answer *no* to all of the above questions and your child continues to cry, consult your pediatrician. If Baby is simply fussy every now and then, we suggest the following techniques to help calm him.

Physical Positions

1. Pick Baby up, hold him tightly over your shoulder, and pat his back.
2. Use Position 1 as you pace.
3. Lay Baby gently across your knees and bounce him rhythmically. Pat him gently on the back.
4. Hold Baby over your arm while he rests on your hip.
5. Put Baby, tummy down, on your lap and push his knees up to his chest.
6. Hold Baby closely and firmly and sit in your rocker and rock, or sit on the edge of a chair and pretend to rock.
7. Hold Baby with his back against your stomach, encircle his waist with your arm, and exert a bit of pressure.

Other Suggestions

1. Swaddle Baby by wrapping him snugly in a light blanket.
2. Give Baby something to suck—a finger, fist, or pacifier. Hold him close and pat his back.
3. Add a ticking clock to the scene; the rhythmic noise can be very soothing.
4. Make the crib smaller by adding a few pillows and stuffed friends. A smaller space is often comforting to Baby.
5. Turn Baby over on his tummy, pull up his cover, and turn on the radio to soft tunes. Pat his back or gently rock his crib.
6. Take Baby for a ride in the car.
7. Put Baby in a front carrier or an umbrella stroller and take a walk around the block.
8. Put Baby in a wind-up swing.
9. Sing to Baby.
10. Whisper in Baby's ear.
11. Take Baby to the mirror so he can see himself; talk to him.
12. Dance with Baby.
13. If Baby finds water soothing, give him a bath, or shower together.

    If nothing works, call for reinforcements and let them try.

APPENDIX B

HAVE BABY, WILL TRAVEL

Many happy moments can be spent traveling with Baby. Day trips to visit friends, museums, or shopping centers are a must for a caregiver with an infant. Keep a travel bag ready to go for these short trips. On longer trips, use the same bag as an airplane, train, or car bag; pack the rest of Baby's things with the family luggage.

Your travel bag should be durable and sturdy. It should have both a handle and shoulder straps. If it is not made of waterproof material, it should at least have several waterproof inside pockets. It should be large enough to easily hold all of Baby's necessities and a small handbag of your own. The following list of essential items for traveling with Baby should be included in your bag. Take only the amount of each that you will really need.

1. Disposable diapers
2. Disposable wipes
3. Diaper cream and powder (buy the sample sizes)
4. A small comb and brush if Baby has enough hair to warrant their use
5. Tissues
6. Plastic zip-lock bags, the larger size
7. Two complete changes of clothes
8. A complete change of outer clothes
9. A small blanket
10. A bib
11. A few small toys
12. Enough food and bottles for the trip

Long-Distance Traveling

Planning for Your Arrival

Be sure to discuss with your host or hostess in advance the kinds of physical arrangements that are to be made for Baby. This will make plans easier for them to complete, and will help you know what to bring.

If the people you are visiting do not have small children, ask them to investigate pediatricians and baby-sitters in advance. Babies always seem to get sick at 3 A.M. in a strange city when you've made no arrangements.

By Airplane

Remember to call the airlines a few days before your departure to tell them that you are traveling with an infant. If they know this, they will usually let you board a little early so that you can get settled without being crowded. Specify any special arrangements you wish to make about food; the flight attendants will generally be happy to warm bottles or baby food for you.

Be sure to get to the airport early. Rushing around at the last minute will leave both you and Baby frazzled and unprepared for the flight. An early arrival will also let you choose your seat. Ask for a seat in the nonsmoking section—healthier and more pleasant for everyone.

By Car

Long car trips with a baby can be difficult for everyone. Try to plan an easy driving schedule that begins early and ends early enough in the afternoon so that everyone can have a rest. Stop frequently.

Even the youngest baby should be securely strapped into a car seat in the back seat. There is a great temptation, particularly on long trips, to let Baby sit in front on someone's lap. This is unsafe and should never be permitted, no matter how fussy Baby gets.

It is wise to pack a cooler in the morning before you leave. Stock it with small containers of prepared food for very young babies, or with peanut butter and jelly sandwiches, cheese and crackers, and fruit for older ones. Remember to bring small containers of juice and milk, and Baby's cup, bottle, and utensils. A large thermos of cool water is a must. Warmed formula can also be kept in a large thermos and poured into bottles when needed.

No Matter How You're Going

—If you plan to be gone any length of time, take a portfolio of Baby's pictures with you. Photos of Baby's house, pets, toys, and friends and admirers are take-alongs that keep him connected with his loved ones.

—A roll of masking tape can provide creative diversions for Baby. This sticky stuff is fun to play with; it is also ideal for retaping disposable diapers.

—A cool washcloth can refresh a wilting baby traveling in hot weather. Simply wrap a dry cloth around an ice cube and place in a zip-lock plastic bag. It will be ready when you are.

—Carrying your young infant in a sling is an easy way to keep your hands free. An umbrella stroller is a good traveling aid for the older baby.

APPENDIX C

FIGHTING THE MEAN MOTHER GUILTS

According to government statistics, only 17 percent of all American families include a father who is the sole breadwinner, a wife who is a full-time homemaker, and one or more children still at home. Nonetheless, this is the stereotype with which most of us have been brought up; many women feel tremendous guilt about working because of it. Here are some things you might want to know that will help you fight the "mean mother guilts" and develop a perspective.

Although current research concerning working mothers and their young children is limited, there have not been any noticeable negative differences between children who spend their day at home and those who spend it in day care. In fact, positive differences have been noted in some testing situations. Children from high-quality care programs were consistently more socially independent, outgoing, task-oriented, and curious. Another important finding contributing to your peace of mind is that the mother-child relationship is not weakened when a child is in day care.

Whether you must work or choose to work, it is important that you feel confident about the care situation you select for your child. There are many kinds of day-care arrangements. No matter which you choose, work hard to develop a relationship of trust and mutual respect with your child's caregivers. Make a real effort to keep the lines of communication open both ways. After all, your child's daily welfare is at stake. The following chart provides a brief comparison of the four basic types of child care and a few thoughts about their advantages and disadvantages.

Type	Advantages	Disadvantages
Baby-sitter in your home	Most convenient Greatest flexibility in terms of hours Will care for a sick child Most individualized care	Hard to locate Not always licensed Most expensive No backup in event of illness No consistent program No social contact(s) for parents
Baby-sitter away from home	Convenient Reasonably flexible hours Will care for a sick child Some individualized care	Hard to locate Not always licensed Expensive No backup in event of illness No consistent program No social contact(s) for parents Sitter may have other household duties
Family group	Convenient Moderately flexible hours Limited number of children lowers cost Some socialization with other babies May have consistent program Some interaction with other parents May be licensed	Usually will *not* accept a sick child No backup in event of illness Other children may not be appropriate playmates

Type	Advantages	Disadvantages
Day-care center	Convenient Maximum dependability regarding services Licensed, trained personnel whose job it is to interact with children Competitively priced Consistent program with planned activities Maximum social interaction with other parents	Least flexibility in hours Center will not accept sick child Larger group size Possible concern over changes in staff

Working outside the home and raising a family, and doing both happily, is very demanding indeed. Here are some tips from working parents we know.

1. Be sure to arrange a special time with your child(ren) each weekend. This should be a time when you are not distracted by anything else. An outing is especially relaxing for both of you—try a walk in the park, a trip to the zoo, a ride around the block in a wagon. In addition, you should arrange a private time—even if it is for only five minutes—to say good-night with a song or a book and a talk with each child each evening.
2. Parents need to have some time alone together; make this one of your priorities.
3. Everyone needs a little time alone, even if it is just to read a magazine for half an hour or to take a nice, hot bath.
4. Subscribing to a working woman's magazine can help fight that feeling of being isolated and burdened.
5. Streamline your housework and learn to live with slightly less than perfectionist standards. Read a book about hints and shortcuts to help reduce your workload.

APPENDIX D

DOWN MEMORY LANE

Name _____

Place of birth _____

Date of birth _____ Day _____ Time _____

Who was present _____

Arrived home for first time _____

Motor Development Milestones

	DATE	COMMENTS
Lifts head	_____	_____
Rolls from back to stomach	_____	_____
Rolls from stomach to back	_____	_____
Rolls completely over	_____	_____
Crawls	_____	_____
Sits alone	_____	_____
Crawls up stairs	_____	_____
Pulls to standing position	_____	_____
Stands alone	_____	_____
Walks alone	_____	_____

Watch Me Grow!

	WEIGHT	LENGTH
1 Month	_____	_____
3 Months	_____	_____
6 Months	_____	_____
12 Months	_____	_____

Feeding Firsts

	DATE	COMMENTS
Begins solids	_____	_____
Drinks from cup	_____	_____
Tries a spoon	_____	_____
Feeds self	_____	_____
Weaned	_____	_____

Cognitive Cuties

	DATE	COMMENTS
Follows objects with eyes	_____	_____
Imitates actions	_____	_____
Points to body parts	_____	_____
Looks for hidden object	_____	_____

Listen to Me!

	DATE	COMMENTS
Vocalizes to get attention	_____	_____
Responds when talked to	_____	_____
Understands name	_____	_____
Understands *no!*	_____	_____
First word	_____	_____

Social Steps

	DATE	COMMENTS
Smiles	_____	_____
Plays peek-a-boo	_____	_____
Teases family	_____	_____
Disturbed by strangers	_____	_____
Gives a kiss or hug	_____	_____

Routine Relief

	DATE	COMMENTS
Sleeps through the night	_____	_____
Splashes, plays, and enjoys bath	_____	_____
Tries to undress self	_____	_____

3637